RISE

OF THE SPIRITUAL ACTIVIST

A BEGINNER'S GUIDE FOR INTEGRATING FAITH AND JUSTICE

GUILLERMO MÁRQUEZ-STERLING

WestBow
PRESS
A DIVISION OF THOMAS NELSON

WestBow Press books may be ordered through booksellers or by contacting:

WestBow Press
A Division of Thomas Nelson
1663 Liberty Drive
Bloomington, IN 47403
www.westbowpress.com
1-(866) 928-1240

Because of the dynamic nature of the Internet, any web addresses or links contained in this book may have changed since publication and may no longer be valid. The views expressed in this work are solely those of the author and do not necessarily reflect the views of the publisher, and the publisher hereby disclaims any responsibility for them.

Any people depicted in stock imagery provided by Thinkstock are models, and such images are being used for illustrative purposes only.

Certain stock imagery © Thinkstock.

ISBN: 978-1-4497-7269-7 (sc)
ISBN: 978-1-4497-7268-0 (hc)
ISBN: 978-1-4497-7397-7 (e)

Library of Congress Control Number: 2012920628

Printed in the United States of America

WestBow Press rev. date: 11/08/2012

CONTENTS

ACKNOWLEDGEMENTS

There is a Celtic prayer that includes the words, "God above me . . . God below me . . . God before me . . . God behind me . . . God all around me . . ." So I will begin by acknowledging God in my thoughts, my words, and my expressions. A close second in my priority of gratitude is my wife, Maria, through whom I have been able to channel the loving Spirit of God. It is only fair to mention next my three grown children, for being more patient with me than I am with them.

Writing a book of this sort is never a solitary process. Although it may seem to the observer that I am alone at the keyboard, there are many voices of "wisdoms past" guiding me as I type. They are, in many ways, the inspiration behind the book: the Rev. Dr. Laurinda Hafner and the Rev. Megan Smith, my colleagues and friends, whose ability to integrate justice into every aspect of their life is truly an inspiration; the late Rev. Chuck Eastman, whose laughter at the arrogance of oppressors taught me about God's sense of ironic justice; the community at Coral Gables Congregational United Church of Christ, who nurtured me through many formative years; Dr. Edith Rasell who introduced me to the hope of economic justice; and finally, every sermon, prayer, or dialogue I listened to and found the tension between faith and justice pulling at my inner core.

I must also acknowledge the many people who work and live activism on a daily basis and whose contribution to humanity is immeasurable. I am especially grateful to Jeannette Smith; Jorge Mursuli; Daniella Levine; Arden Shank; Carol Krech; Noel Cleland; and David Lawrence Jr. They agreed to be interviewed by me, and that alone has filled me with enough gratitude to make me teary eyed. A special word of appreciation is extended to Patty Shillington, my editor, whose sharp eye and word genius is beyond measure. Finally, I thank you, the reader. Without the hope of your reading and using this book to create positive change in the world, I never would have broached this topic.

PREFACE

In 1985 I moved to Miami as a young man full of hopes and dreams for a life and home with my beloved. Back then, Miami was a hard city. Racial tensions were palpable. Cocaine cowboys were a violent, high-flying fixture against a backdrop of economic inequality and despair. An egocentric culture of "me-first" ruled the morning commute and infected every aspect of life. After graduating from the local state university, I worked for eight years as a public school teacher. My quest for spiritual enlightenment took me through an interesting journey, and in hindsight it seems as if I'd been led to the church I have grown to call my spiritual home.

The United Church of Christ (UCC) is a justice-oriented church with a distinct love for the arts, a welcoming community, and a progressive theology. When Miami was awash in a sea of conservative thinkers and fundamentalist churches, the UCC was one of the progressive voices. While most Miami churches constituted an obstacle to human rights, the UCC was an advocating presence. The refreshingly progressive culture in this church allowed human rights advocates in South Florida to become curious about it and to visit it Sunday after Sunday. Consequently, the church created a community that was colored with the best progressive minds of South Florida. That I should have been so fortunate to find this church, to have been embraced by it and to have developed under its tutelage is more than good fortune. It's the tangible outcome of following the guiding voice of God.

Spiritual Activist Jeannette Smith offered in her interview, "We may not be able to change the world, but we certainly can do something about our little corner." This little corner of the nation has a unique history with injustice. Miami is far from the halls of politics in Washington, DC, but it is in the very center of inequality. Millionaires from around the world travel to Miami-Dade County to purchase waterfront homes. The richest zip code in the nation is a ferry boat away from homeless people wandering through Miami's inner city.

Consequently, it is no surprise that this city should also be home to the most gifted collection of activists. Over the years, my presence in the church has afforded me the opportunity to develop friendships and relationships with many wonderful people who possess a deep understanding of love and justice. They are the activists who stand against injustice and who look to collaborate with the faith community. When I first started writing this book in the summer of 2011, I had a notion that I should interview different activists throughout our nation. Then, one night, the obvious question came to me: Why travel the country in search of activists when such an intense concentration of them are living and working here in Miami? It is to my professional benefit that most of these activists pass by the UCC at one point or another. I offer their voice throughout the book, fully aware that they provide a deeper lesson than anything I can write. Their connection between faith and justice is refreshing and inspiring.

This book is being completed before the 2012 presidential elections, which may prove to be the ultimate battle between conservatives and progressives. It is upsetting to hear the irrational, fear-based rhetoric directed against President Obama and to witness political efforts trying to undo many civil rights of women and minorities. It is disturbing to hear the rhetoric aimed at universities and colleges for doing exactly what they were built to do: expand the minds of the students. However, nothing is more alarming to me than the fact that average, middle-class people have become followers of such negative and wrongful political strategies. When I hear crowds cheering wrongful opinions that promote fear, ignorance, and violence, I have to recognize the power of wrongful rhetoric. I listen to their applause and I ask, "Do they know what they are applauding?" It seems to me these people are, at best, confused about the boundaries between faith and spirituality, public policy, and religious institutions.

When I was in my late twenties and working as a ninth grade public school teacher, I witnessed a violent episode that was the result of racial tension between the local African American girls and the newly arrived Latina girls. By the end of the violent altercation, three girls were taken to the emergency room, one with an avulsed breast from a human bite. Surprisingly, the fight was instigated by one of the teachers, an African American woman who oversaw the cheerleading program. She was removed from her teaching post, but the damage to the school's community seemed irreparable. In the aftermath of the fight, the racial tensions were as palpable as the sweat on my brow.

The school principal brought in a consultant to work with the faculty on conflict resolution. The homeroom period was extended by eight minutes so every teacher would have a daily opportunity to address the racial tension in a constructive manner. I did not have a homeroom period, so I joined a veteran teacher whose wisdom reflected an innate intelligence and years of teaching in an inner-city school. The veteran teacher led the students to find common ground and to realize the anger they felt had nothing to do with each other but with the poverty surrounding their lives. She spoke to the students about the Rev. Dr. Martin Luther King Jr. and taught them a new song—new to them but well-known to older generations—"We Shall Overcome." By the end of the school year, African American and Latino students were united against the ills of poverty and discrimination.

I learned a lot from that veteran schoolteacher. It was my first encounter with a spiritual activist. Nearly twenty years have passed since that violent episode. I realize now how small it was in comparison with the many stabbings and riots other schools have experienced. Yet it was significant enough to set an entire school on a healing process that would change the lives of students and faculty.

Shortly thereafter I entered the ministry and began walking down a path that led me to some amazing people doing amazing work. Like that veteran teacher, they helped me dig deeper and become aware of the real issues underlying the violence in our lives.

In my many years of serving as a pastor, I have come across people with a deep desire to improve the lives of others but with no idea as to how this should be done. Too often they give up, thinking the problem is too big and they are too small. It has been my vocation to encourage those people, for any effort they do is part of a larger solution. This book is an extension of that vocation. Recognizing that there are entire university programs on social change, and that one book alone cannot pretend to cover all the issues, this book is designed as a starting point for the person who is searching for the connection between faith and social change. Although I am a Christian pastor, I deliberately write to the larger community, to people of all faiths who have the potential to be spiritual activists. The book uses language that is inclusive of a universal God so any person, from any walk of life, can be inspired to connect the Spirit of God with social change. It is my hope that the book will inspire you, the reader, to live a life that is intentionally generous and justice oriented. It is my hope that you will become a leader who will bring about positive change toward a greater good. It is my hope that you mentor younger people about the real issues underlying the violence in our lives.

INTRODUCTION

Watch your thoughts; they become words.
Watch your words; they become actions. Watch your actions;
they become habit. Watch your habits; they become character.
Watch your character; it becomes your destiny.

-Lao Tzu

The 1990s were a challenging decade for humanitarian workers around the world. It was a decade marked by genocides in two continents, of global atrocities and blatant injustices. In April 1994 the country of Rwanda was torn apart by an ethnic competition between the Hutu and the Tutsi tribes. This led to the mass murders of more than eight hundred thousand people in a four-month period. The war in Rwanda was by far the most brutal effort to cleanse an entire ethnic group since the Holocaust of World War II. While the Hutus were terrorizing the Tutsi, the Bosnian Serbs were systematically eliminating the Bosnian Croats and Bosnian Muslims. From 1992 to 1995, the Serbian army led a campaign of ethnic cleansing that included rape, murder, unlawful confinement, and deportation. In both wars, the international community had to intervene. These crimes against humanity raise many questions about the promotion of wrongful and violent ideas in organized social systems.

Knowing that such violence does not erupt overnight, how was the stage set for rational people to justify the killing of men and women, children and elderly? How many community leaders gave speeches and sermons that planted seeds of hate and discrimination, eventually growing into violent acts of hate? Can this rhetoric be identified to prevent the emergence of wrongful leaders with wrongful intentions that might lead an entire country into a genocidal war? Where else could this happen? Are there people and organizations in the United Sates promoting similar discrimination?

Developed and modern nations learned how discrimination can lead to blatant injustice, murder, and even genocide. Yet if we listen with discerning ears, we can recognize discrimination today in the speeches of community leaders that might lead to violent and regrettable actions. In March 2012, at a rally for presidential hopeful Rick Santorum, in a room with hundreds of people and before a countless audience watching on television, the Rev. Dennis Terry called for a Christian nation and the removal of non-Christians from America. This is language that fertilizes the ground for discriminatory legislation and justifies persecution as God's will. Consider that Reverend Terry's audience included people lacking the mental strength to discern which ideas should never be acted upon. Such mentally unstable people are living and walking among us all the time. Every community has them, including Reverend Terry's audience. Consider a plausible chain of events that take a member of Reverend Terry's audience from listener to actor, from passive citizen to promoter of xenophobia, from living in harmony with a diverse community to actively making people who are different feel unwelcome. From peaceful to violent.

There can be no doubt that violent people are among us, waiting for the wrong public speaker to push them into regrettable action. We only need to remember April 19, 1995, and the bombing of the Alfred P. Murrah Federal Building in downtown Oklahoma City by Timothy McVeigh and Terry Nichols. More recently, on January 8, 2011, there was the shooting by Jared Lee Loughner of US Representative Gabrielle Gifford and six other innocent victims, including a nine-year-old child. These deaths are to be differentiated from the more common street side shooting or crimes of passion in that they targeted a government official, forcing us to reexamine the genesis of such actions. Where does it all begin? It all begins with a word—specifically, a wrongful word. Unfortunately, violent people are among us, and every public speaker has to consider that they may part of his audience. Consequently, public speakers must know the power of words.

During the 2008 presidential race and in the years that followed, there were multiple reports of people screaming irrational insults at President Obama. As we witnessed the violence-laced language the protesters hurled, many citizens feared our president would suffer at the hands of a crazed gunman. In the same manner that a sailboat relies on the wind for its motion, a violent person is stimulated by fear-based rhetoric that propels him forward. In the spirit of concern, we must examine several questions: What are the influential forces that lead to the violence of any tragic event? What type of environment is society promoting, and how is that environment affecting us all? Is society getting better, or is it creating more anxiety and negative emotions? I propose that society as a whole has to share some degree of responsibility for the violent acts of any individual. Like it or not, there were influential forces that led McVeigh and Loughner to their carefully planned acts of violence. The connection between wrongful rhetoric and wrongful actions cannot be denied, regardless of arguments that attempt to evade this responsibility. It is my theory that elements in our modern society are promoting ideas that generate anxiety, fear, and, ultimately, violence.

In the last fifteen years we have witnessed a rise of the Wrongful Activist. The Wrongful Activist is a person who promotes an idea or behavior that by any measure is wrong and harmful to the lives of others. Sometimes this person is a commentator, a religious leader, a political hopeful, or a celebrity who promotes her wrongful agenda while giving speeches that move people into wrongful thinking and wrongful action. When the Wrongful Activist is examined from any lens, be it Christian, Jewish, Muslim, Buddhist or Humanist, his words are recognized as wrong. The Wrongful Activist taps into the violent, sinful, and wrongful pools that dwell in every human being, bringing out the lower qualities of humanity. Consequently, there is a tangible fear that emotionally unbalanced individuals will be fueled by the words of a Wrongful Activist, and violence will ensue. But hope exists because there are people who stand up to what is wrong. They are the Spiritual Activists.

For the sake of clarity, it is important that we comprehend certain terms in the same manner. Too often people think they are saying the same things but do not realize the context behind the listeners provides a different understanding. For example, the word "liberal" can be used by political conservatives as an insult. For others, it is a simple description of economic strategies while political progressives wear that title as a badge of honor. We may experience the same range of responses when using the word "spiritual." So what do we mean by the words activist and spiritual? Is there a difference between being spiritual and religious? What is the difference between a regular activist, a Spiritual Activist and a Wrongful Activist? Keep these questions in mind as we peel away the layers that reveal the complexity of spiritual activism. This book aims to develop the description of two forms of activism: Spiritual and Wrongful. I propose that the best way to counter the influences of a Wrongful Activist is through a spiritual re-awakening in the activist movement. The time is now for the Spiritual Activist.

In most political and economic negotiations, a lot of work occurs behind the scenes. Often the real players in a political process do not want to be seen, and television viewers only receive a snapshot of the handshake between the two competing leaders. But as negotiations are hammered out, whose interest is being spoken for? This is an important question to raise and examine, for it keeps our leaders accountable. The responsibility of every citizen is to examine the deals made in political or economic negotiations to see who benefits. Unfortunately, most people just accept the twenty-second headline from the morning news show, thus avoiding responsibility by claiming ignorance.

The philosophical question of responsibility has been visited by several scholars. How much responsibility does a community bear for the actions of its political leader? In his article "The Responsibility of Intellectuals," Noam Chomsky reexamines that question,[1] first posed by Dwight Macdonald after World War II. When the world was pointing an accusatory finger at the German people for the atrocities committed by the Nazi government, Macdonald examined the community's responsibility for the actions of its leaders. Some twenty years later Chomsky redirects the question as the responsibility of intellectuals. He states, "Intellectuals are in a position to expose the lies of government . . . to speak the truth." In this book I build upon Macdonald and Chomsky's words by placing the mantle of responsibility on the activist.

An activist, in order to be effective, must become the "Chomsky intellectual" and receive the training to seek the truth hidden behind the distorted veil of a twenty-second headline in the morning news. An activist is a person who wants to create systemic change in order to reach a specific goal for a specific population. Activists are usually fueled by humanist ideals and historically have proven to be necessary for the development of society. Many historical figures were the intellectuals and activists of their time. People such as John Adams, Thomas Jefferson, and Benjamin Franklin found ways of leading a movement that eventually led to the War of Independence and the formation of the United States of America. The list of people who stood up to injustice is extensive and includes names such as Cesar Chavez, Susan B. Anthony, Harvey Milk, Angela Davis, and many others. Although many activists have caused reforms, an activist is not necessarily a reformer. A person who works with the system from inside it, to create change in said system, is a reformer. Too often, reformers are part of the problem because they are part of the system. At one point, a conflict of interest will arise that renders reformers ineffective in bringing about the necessary change. An activist usually works from outside the system and is willing to topple it in order to bring about change. When the people in power realize what is at stake, they take the activist seriously and begin to cooperate.

A Spiritual Activist is an individual who has much in common with a secular activist, but this individual is fueled by her understanding of what God requires. A Spiritual Activist understands that the pursuit of justice is another spiritual discipline or expression of his relationship with God. It is common for Spiritual Activists to speak about their relationship with God, and how that relationship led to an inner transformation. It is from this faith based understanding that the Spiritual Activist is propelled to undo the wrongs that surround us. The list of spiritual activists includes people such as Harriet Tubman, Mohandas K. Gandhi, Rev. Dr. Martin Luther King Jr., Coretta Scott King, Julia Ward Howe, Rabbi Abraham Joshua Heschel, Rev. Dr. William Sloan Coffin Jr., and many others.

Why Spiritual Activism?

For far too many decades there has been an intentional effort of separating faith from activism. Too many people believe there need not be a relationship between the spiritual/religious life and the political and economic world. This separation is a consequence of people observing how the conservative religious organizations in the world have used and manipulated God to promote wrongful ideas and wrongful policies. Because too often God is wrongfully used to justify a social position, a growing population has responded by removing spirituality from the activist conversation. In either scenario, God being manipulated or God being pushed out, the winner is the Wrongful Activist, for it feeds an argument that many people will follow. Consequently, the Spiritual Activist must reclaim faith loudly and unashamedly. If progressive activists would connect justice with God, maybe more people would stand up to the intimidating forces that lead to wrongful policies and actions in our nation and around the world.

Before I discuss the term "Wrongful Activist," let us look at the word spiritual, since it is often used in conflicting ways. First of all, do not confuse spiritual with religious. There are many religious people who lack an ounce of spirituality, and conversely there are many spiritual people who do not subscribe to any particular religion. However, many religions around the world have a deep spiritual understanding and promote spirituality and mysticism. Secondly, let us not fall into the trap of comparing forms of spirituality and ascribing value to them. This only leads to the harmful division and injustices that have marked human history.

For the sake of simplicity, I am defining the word spiritual as a universal, human attribute to seek a worldview and guidance from a Divine Source or Supreme Being that transcends human understanding. This Supreme Being is commonly referred to as God but in other languages might be called Yahweh, Elohim, or Allah. In the Christian tradition this Supreme Being often has been referred to as God the Father. The feminist and womanist movements of the twentieth century have helped expand our views about the attributes of God, making them more inclusive. The snowball effect has led to groups of people moving away from using the word "God" altogether. They prefer other titles, such as Higher Power, Holy One, and Divine Creator. More inclusive movements may refer to God as the Universe. Regardless of semantics, a Spiritual Activist will search for wisdom, guidance, and strength from a Divine Source that is understood as loving, forgiving, positive, and transcendent. For cultural reasons, in this book I will refer to this Divine Source as God and I will use inclusive language.

I recognize that the word "God" stirs up negative connotations for some people, especially those who are moving toward atheism. They reject the traditional anthropomorphic view of a god who is a supreme being, omnipotent and all controlling, sitting in judgment of humanity to bring about "the rapture" at the end of times. For the record, I also reject that image. The God I believe in and will promote does not possess human qualities and is in everything and of everything. This God is the essence of life, love, and harmony. This view of a panentheistic God promotes that God is everywhere. My view of God is like Dr. Marcus Borg's analogy of a fish in a bowl of water.[2] The fish is in water and the water is in the fish. The fish does not differentiate between water that is in it and water that is around it. Likewise, humans are in God, of God, and surrounded by God like fish are in water. To be spiritual is to be aware of the waters of God as we swim and live in these waters.

To be spiritual necessitates a connection and a relationship with the Spirit of God. Here the waters become less clear, for there is no formula to measure such a connection. How do we distinguish a person who is spiritual from a person who is not? How can we measure the degrees of spirituality? The answers to these questions are debatable, but for the most part, a spiritual person does not claim that virtue. Spirituality is lived but never fully achieved. It is a lifelong pursuit of enlightenment that might be momentarily reached but never fully grasped. Being spiritual is about developing a connection with the Spirit of God that is always beyond us, and it is about connecting with our neighbors in a manner that recognizes and honors their rightful place in God's creation.

Consequently, to be spiritual is to be humble. Tenzin Gyatso, the fourteenth Dalai Lama of Tibet, wrote, "Whenever I interact with someone, may I view myself as the lowest amongst all, and, from the very depths of my heart, respectfully hold others as superior."[3] In this verse, the Dalai Lama teaches humility as one of the highest attributes in the pursuit of spiritual enlightenment. It teaches us that spirituality is practiced with humility, a quality lost in today's world. Humility is the intentional practice of respecting and elevating the other person out of love for his divine attributes. Humility is not to be confused with low self-esteem. On the contrary, the humble person has a healthy self-esteem that allows her to practice humility. To be humble is a choice. To have low self-esteem is a condition. Humility is an acquired and learned worldview. Spirituality and humility go hand in hand, for the spiritual person is aware that all human accomplishments are insignificant when compared to God's creation.

Being spiritual is not necessarily synonymous with being religious. A religious person is one who expresses his belief in God through the vehicle of organized religion. The institution of the church, synagogue, temple, or mosque provides a setting for this person to express and further his faith. Being religious means you subscribe to the doctrines of the religious institution and you practice your faith in the manner the religious institution teaches. For example, many Christians take Holy Communion in their church on Sunday mornings, and many Jews fast on Yom Kippur, the Day of Atonement. Ideally speaking, the people who practice these religious rites experience a spiritual connection to God through them, but some people don't. Some people just go through the motions without connecting to the Spirit of God. Consequently, being religious does not automatically equate to being spiritual.

Both activism and spirituality are deep subjects in and of themselves. To become an effective activist requires academic study, field training, and mentoring. To live a spiritual life, one must integrate academic studies with mindfulness and certain disciplines, as well as mentoring. Therefore, the spiritual activist is not made overnight. Spiritual activism requires years of study and a faith that is practiced with intention. The spiritual activist need not be a religious person, but many are.

This book is meant to help the reader discern between spiritual and wrongful activists. It will serve as a beginner's manual and guide to develop the skills and attributes needed to be a spiritual activist. It will provide a step-by-step description for pursuing justice, as well as narratives from activists who have worked in the field. This book does not promote the theology of one particular religion, be it Christian, Jewish, Buddhist, Muslim, etc., yet it builds on what they have in common. Ultimately, this book is meant to help the reader consider how to be spiritual and an agent of justice.

PART I
THE PHILOSOPHY OF SPIRITUAL ACTIVISM

What does the LORD require of you? To act justly and
to love mercy and to walk humbly with your God.

~Micah 6:8b

All it takes is one person . . . and another . . .
and another . . . and another . . . to start a movement.

~Abraham Joshua Heschel

CHAPTER 1

Spiritual versus Religious

A friendly study of the world's religions is a sacred duty.
                                        ~Mohandas Gandhi

Because religious discrimination does exist, and because many people are hostile toward those who are different, it is important to develop an inclusive perspective and see beyond religious differences. Love is the universal vehicle for all religions, and justice is the common ground. A Spiritual Activist seeks to build bridges and form coalitions with people of various faiths. This can happen only if there is understanding and a willingness to work together.

In this chapter I will briefly explore four world religions: Judaism, Christianity, Islam, and Buddhism and their venerated spiritual leaders. In the sacred texts of these religions, each leader is considered either to be divine or to have had an encounter with the divine. From a secular point of view, they are considered historical figures whose work ignited a movement and changed the world. Each focused on ways to liberate their people from an oppressive force or condition. It is important to recognize that other influential thinkers and factors contributed to the development and evolution of these religions. For brevity's sake I will only examine the founding leaders of these religions. I encourage you, the reader, to study these four religions and their venerated leaders in greater depth.

Moses and Judaism

Judaism's gift to the world is that of the prophet, the person who demands justice in the name of God. There are many prophets in the sacred Judaic texts, but Moses is the most venerated prophet in traditional Judaism. According to the book of Exodus, Moses was the liberator of the Jewish people who were held captive in Egypt around the year 1350 BCE (Before the Common Era).[4] He is described as having committed murder after witnessing the mistreatment of a Jewish slave by an Egyptian guard. In fear for his life, he fled. After a long journey of several years, he came to experience God at the top of Mount Horeb. In this God experience, Moses was transformed and he understood that he had to lead the struggle against the political and military forces in Egypt.[5] Although many modern scholars dispute the miraculous and fantastical stories that surround the person of Moses, none dispute the historical facts about the enslaved Jewish people in Egypt and their liberation by him. The bondage identified in the book of Exodus was a physical one. Communities that have experienced similar oppression find the stories of Moses an inspiration that fuels their liberation movements. It is interesting to note that although Moses cannot be identified as a pacifist; his manner of dealing with the Egyptian pharaoh was peaceful and assertive, which teaches us that peaceful negotiations and assertiveness are not new strategies for those who seek liberation.

Buddha and Buddhism

Siddhartha Gautama, also known as the Buddha Gautama, was a man who lived in Nepal and Northern India roughly in the year 550 BCE. His life story and teachings have been chronicled in the *Dhammapada*, the *Sutta-Nipâta,* and several other sacred books. His search for enlightenment led to an understanding of liberation from the oppression created by the human condition. The bondage described by the Buddha Gautama is an internal one that can be overcome only by reaching an enlightened stage. Although the Buddha Gautama taught that suffering is part of the human condition, the search for enlightenment eventually leads people to detach from the conditions and behaviors that create suffering. Buddhism is considered a nontheistic religion. Leading scholars of Buddhism do not make an effort to renounce or embrace God. The closest theistic terminology Buddhism utilizes is that of "original consciousness." The Buddha Gautama promoted peace and nonviolence, teaching his listeners to follow the Eightfold Noble Path: right understanding, right thought, right speech, right action, right livelihood, right effort, right mindfulness, and right concentration. In theory, if entire communities were to follow the Eightfold Noble Path with integrity, the probability of relating to one another with fairness and respect would increase

3

to a tipping point at which human suffering would significantly decrease and enlightenment would be accessible to more people.

Jesus and Christianity

From a secular point of view, Jesus was an activist. From a Christian point of view, Jesus is divine. Regardless of your view, the fact remains that he was a man who sought to liberate Jewish people in first-century Israel from the oppressive temple laws and doctrines that promoted a view of a judgmental and vindictive God. The bondage described is theological, for the people felt oppressed by the religious interpretation of the Pharisees and the Sadducees, the ruling religious leaders in first-century Jerusalem. Jesus spoke about the promise of God's realm as being within, not in the Mosaic laws. His teachings had a nonviolent focus and were highly revolutionary, for they promoted an internal freedom. Jesus was Jewish, as were his followers. These first-century activists were not out to form a new religion, but their revolutionary understanding of God led to a Jewish (and non-Jewish) movement to peaceably resist the military forces of the Roman Empire and the religious rule of the Jewish temple. Eventually, this movement led to the popular formation of Christianity and to it becoming the official religion of the Roman Empire in the third-century CE. Some scholars argue that it was at that moment that Christianity began to lose its way. Regardless of what may have occurred in the institution of the Christian religion, the historical Jesus is regarded as a man whose guiding principles, lifestyle, and teachings created a movement that became a tangible threat to the Jewish temple and the Roman Empire.

Muhammad and Islam

According to the various *siras* (biographies of Muhammad), in the year 610 CE, Muhammad, a learned man with many talents, entered a cave to meditate. It was there where he received a message from the Angel Gabriel. Thus began the Prophet Muhammad's difficult and dangerous journey to unite the different tribes of Arabia under the message, "God is one." Islamic tradition teaches that the Angel Gabriel recited a message from God to the Prophet Muhammad over a twenty-three-year period. The Prophet Muhammad then recited that message, word for word, to his followers. This message was written down in the Quran, which means "recitation." Consequently, the Quran is believed by Islamic people to be the literal word of God.

The Prophet Muhammad was an activist in that he sought to liberate the people from the oppression caused by division. This was a bondage of chaos, division, tribal warfare, and competing ideologies. By uniting under one leader and theology, the many Arabian tribes were able to become a stronger nation. Muhammad's quest of unification was successful, and by the time of his death in 632 CE, most of the Arabian Peninsula had united under the religion of Islam. Although Muhammad was not a pacifist, the pursuit of peace was central to his teachings. The Quran teaches that peacemaking is a godly act worthy of praise and reward.[6]

Spiritual Activism versus Institutionalized Religion

These four great religious leaders—Moses, Siddhartha Gautama, Jesus, and Muhammad—were men of amazing principles and drive. They all have several things in common. First, they were men in a deep relationship with God and lived and practiced spiritual disciplines that fostered that relationship. Second, they were educated men. This in itself may not seem like an achievement in today's world, where education is promoted freely, but we must take a look at the context and realize that fewer than 1 percent of the population could read and write during those times. This is significant because it creates a correlation between education and justice. Third, each of these leaders worked outside the established power structure. They were activists, not reformers. Fourth, but certainly not last, each man valued peace. This last point will create some controversy among pacifists, for both Moses and Muhammad were military leaders. However, despite this military history, they were men who promoted peace as a central doctrine in their religion and at different times practiced peaceful methodologies to achieve their goal. Although our modern understanding of nonviolence was visible in the lives of Jesus and the Buddha Gautama, nonviolence was valued by Moses and Muhammad and currently by leaders in these respective religions.

It is important to acknowledge the significant differences between these four men and the religions that followed them. If we study the institutionalized religion and contrast it to the life of the leading founder, we will inevitably come across contradictions between the two. This is due to the fact that everything is in constant flux, and no single religion is ever immune to change. Change is the true constant. The challenge is to make those writings and sacred teachings relevant to new generations, who are often the promoters of change.

The Rev. Dr. Martin Luther King Jr. was an activist who came from the institution of the Christian church (as lived in the southern African American community) to promote justice for all people in the United States. King reinterpreted many of the sacred texts in the old and new testaments of the Judeo/Christian Bible to inspire the civil rights movement, and it was the community of the church that provided him the foundation upon which he stood. The Rev. Dr. William Sloan Coffin Jr. was able to utilize the institution of the Christian church (as lived in the Anglo-New England community) to promote justice during the civil rights movement. Both pastors were working the same issue from different geographical locations to achieve the same goal. Both pastors were activists with a deep understanding of God's call for justice.

Even though these two pastors used the church as their vehicle for spiritual activism, a Spiritual Activist may have to work outside the institution of religion in order to get results. Invariably, religious institutions have, as one of their main priorities, the preservation of the institution and its assets. This creates a conflict of interest for the institution, which at one point or another will have to choose between practicing the core values taught in its sacred texts and preserving the institution's assets. For example, religious institutions have monetary investments they protect and grow. This goal is often in conflict with the core value of ending poverty. Since it is impossible to serve two masters (a universal lesson in several traditions), it becomes difficult for these institutions to proclaim integrity when facing this issue.

Another example of this conflict is the institutionalization of sexism. In the four religions described, sexism is active and promoted by internal policies. Yet all four religions can point to texts in their sacred writings that promote equality and fairness between the sexes. Consequently, as a Spiritual Activist you may find the institution of your chosen religion to not have the ability, or the will, to cooperate with the activism and justice you seek to create.

So What Is One to Do?

If you are realizing there might be a conflict between organized religion and spiritual activism, you do not have to renounce your religious affiliation, but you do have to examine how your core values will be compatible (or not) with your house of worship. Your religion of birth does not need to determine your lifelong expression of faith. Many people are raised in one faith, and when they mature, they make an intentional decision to follow another. If there is a conflict between your religious affiliation and your spiritual beliefs, and you feel conflicted about it, consider the following options:

1. Realize there is a big difference between God and organized religion. God is much larger than any structure humans can create. God is beyond any human description. Consequently, stay away from doctrines that equate God with the institution of religion. This realization might help you be forgiving of the limitations you find in your house of worship.

2. Realize that not all houses of worship are equipped to be part of a spiritual activist movement. Utilize your house of worship as a center for prayer and worship that will feed your soul and replenish your energy for the good fight that spiritual activism will demand of you.

3. Search for a new house of worship that will be more compatible with your justice core values. For example, if you are seeking justice for the gay and lesbian community, you may want to attend a house of worship that is not homophobic.

All human institutions are flawed because humanity is deeply flawed. These institutions seek higher ideals but at times do not know how to reach them. The Spiritual Activist is a person whose message seeks to create a movement for change, and this may or may not include a house of worship. Certain institutions will never change, and others will become great allies in the struggle.

CHAPTER 2

Why Do We Need
Spiritual Activists?

All that we are is the result of what we have thought.
The mind is everything. What we think—we become.

~Buddha Gautama

Our postmodern society sets young people on a path to live their lives on the surface. It is depressing to see the number of people who are more concerned about the piercing on their belly button than about the meaning and purpose of their life. It is infuriating to see the number of children who have less than acceptable levels of education and grow up to be unemployable adults. It is so disappointing to witness the number of people who equate video games with human interaction, charity with justice, capitalism with human rights, and God with nation.

Yet there is a growing awareness that something is missing, and more people are searching for meaning and purpose. These are people who realize the technological advances of the last decade might be entertaining but do very little to improve the quality of life in their working-class neighborhoods. These are people who have lost their jobs, their homes, and their well-being while the wealthy grow richer and the government becomes more contentious. The people are thirsty for hope, but in what and whom? Here is where the Spiritual Activist is needed to remind them that the Spirit of God is within and among them, fueling their inspiration to stand together against the powers that oppress. The Spiritual Activist organizes the community while promoting ideals that teach compassion, peace, fairness, well-being, and balance for all people. Ultimately, meaning and hope reside in human relationships that transcend money and gadgets.

The Wrong Form of Activism

Now is a time of growing discontent, when voices are seeking to be heard. Leaders are needed to unite these voices not for the benefit of a political party but for the welfare of humanity. The people are searching for this leader. They are eager to place the mantle on a person, or on an organization, that will help them. This eagerness makes them vulnerable to individuals who can manipulate them by tossing out a few "tag lines" that ring true but lack the deeper values of compassion, fairness, peace, and peacemaking. These manipulative leaders use violent and hateful rhetoric that incites violence and hatred. When people who have not received proper education or spiritual development, and might also be emotionally imbalanced, listen and follow a manipulative leader, they can easily find themselves committing an act they might later regret . . . one the whole world regrets.

Between the years 2008 and 2010, many people were aghast at the wrongful behavior that was spreading across the United States. It was painful to see how mobs were screaming insults at President Obama and disrupting his speeches. He was called the Anti-Christ, Adolf Hitler, a socialist, a communist—and in the spirit of insult, the president was called a Muslim, which is really not an insult. It could be argued that there have always been people who disagree with their elected president as well as people who strongly dislike (or even hate) members of the opposite political party. But it is difficult to make the case that the intensity and frequency of the current wave of wrongful behavior has always existed. Something has changed in the landscape: the rise of the Wrongful Activist.

The Wrongful Activist has been with us since the beginning of time. An extreme example of a Wrongful Activist would be Adolf Hitler, whose ideas led Germany to war and caused the death of more than forty million civilians from war-related acts, disease, and famine. In the United States, wrongful activism led to the persecution of many innocent people. Senator Joseph McCarthy, the leader of McCarthyism and the Red Scare, was a Wrongful Activist who convinced a nation that persecuting innocent lives was in the best interest of the community. The Ku Klux Klan, another extreme example of wrongful activism, is able to convince people that God demands they commit acts of violence against people of color and non-Christian religions. It seems bizarre, but we still can find organizations today that promote such wrongful ideologies.

The Wrongful Activist is often disguised as a political strategist, town sheriff, news commentator, radio/TV personality or film director. In the last fifteen years, many Wrongful Activists have been getting wealthy from their soapbox, and consequently more people are drawn to that activity in the hopes of making significant wealth. Many Wrongful Activists have been able to exercise a certain amount of power by influencing the political process and human behavior. They promote bias, discrimination, and fear, leading people to shameful acts of persecution they think fall under the protection of the US Constitution. For several years now there has been a resurgence of the Wrongful Activist and consequently a rise of wrongful behavior.

Wrongful Words Contaminate the Soul

The negative energy created by the Wrongful Activist enters the psyche of the people, and fertilizes the soil of violence with hateful discourse. Wrongful Activists will quickly evade responsibility for the actions that followed their discourse, but people who believe in the energies of the spiritual realm will correlate the two with sound argument. These are not fly-by-night quacks, or dime-store tarot card readers. Theologians and venerated teachers of all major religions have addressed the energy created by thought and language. This is an important connection for everyone to understand. I encourage my readers to deepen their knowledge on this issue by approaching their religious leader or teacher and ask about the connection between the human soul and language.

Study the energy behind the spoken word and you will comprehend what I offer now in the following simile/metaphor:

Words are like stones that are tossed into the pond of our being. They make a splash upon impact, and waves of energy can be seen in the ripples that disrupt the surface. The soul is like a pond. It has an ecosystem of its own and a complexity that is wondrous to contemplate. When a word or image is tossed at the soul, it makes an impact and then vanishes almost immediately, just like a stone disappearing under the water, but the effect of the word remains in the being of the listener. It creates ripples of energy, which in turn disrupt other thoughts and feelings. If the words are compatible with the ecosystem of the soul, these become part of its harmonious existence.

Consider wrongful words like stones dipped in toxic substances. When a toxic stone is tossed into a pond, not only does it make the usual splash and ripples, as it lies at the bottom of the pond it poisons the waters. The pond has its natural agents to combat poisonous elements, and if the toxic stone is small and solitary the pond may be able to effectively eliminate those toxins. But if toxic stones are tossed in numbers too large for the pond to combat, the level of toxicity will overcome the pond and its death ensues.

When a Wrongful Activist tosses wrongful words into the very big pond of society, they are poisonous to the wellbeing of society. The pond of society is more like an ocean, so when wrongful words are spoken in one region, other regions remain unaffected. In recent years, the Wrongful Activists have been using the vehicles of TV, radio, Internet and blog sites. Communicating over such media multiplies the number of listeners exponentially. Consequently, in today's world the Wrongful Activist can create train-loads of toxic, wrongful words and dump them into the collective psyche of the people. The splash generated by these words constantly being hurled at the water has created tidal waves of disruption that erode the shores of our lives. Most importantly, the toxic element being introduced is poisonous to the soul of the people, and it is changing what once was a civil society into contentious and dysfunctional mobs full of hatred and animosity.

The chain of events between wrongful words and wrongful action may not be arguable in a court of law, but in the eyes of a Spiritual Activist there is a direct correlation. It is a weak argument when the person tossing the stone evades responsibility by claiming it was the stone that disrupted the water. Likewise, it is a weak argument when Wrongful Activists evade responsibility for the wrongful behavior exhibited by mobs of people or by solitary gunmen who were influenced by their wrongful words.

Unfortunately, we are surrounded by Wrongful Activists. They often hide behind sparkling smiles, expensive outfits and good makeup. Most are unaware of their wrongful message and are products of a larger system. To identify a Wrongful Activist requires careful listening and discernment. In today's world, these are much-needed skills. The identifying marks of the Wrongful Activist are the following:

1. Uses Violent Imagery that Promotes Violence.

A Wrongful Activist will compare himself to a violent animal such as a pit bull or a grizzly bear. Metaphorical language that is directly connected to instruments of violence can be easily heard in his rhetoric. Often the Wrongful Activist is not even aware of his language and in self-defense will claim it was not meant to be understood in that manner. This is the defense of ignorance, for the Wrongful Activist is not aware of the violence that is imbedded in his worldview. Years of wrongful living, wrongful thinking, and wrongful speaking have led to his use of violent language in a very natural manner. The Wrongful Activist does not know how to convey a message in any other manner. Listen carefully and you will be able to identify a Wrongful Activist by the use of words and images that are inherently violent.

2. Lacks Compassion, Is Bigoted, and Attacks the Innocent.

A Wrongful Activist can be heard making fun of people who are different. Not too long ago I heard a television commentator poking fun at a transgender person. The irresponsibility of that commentator is unforgivable due to the fact that his audience exceeded a million viewers. Such a comment only reinforces negative stereotypes and will promote more discrimination toward transgender people.

A Wrongful Activist will also make fun of people for the sake of her goals. In September 2009, four widows of the 9/11 attack were described as "witches" because their petition ran counter to the political agenda of the Wrongful Activist. This attack on a group of women who are clearly identified as victims is blatantly wrong and many have stood up to say so. The question must be asked, "How can any person not see that speaking such words is wrong?" The answer requires a spiritual understanding of how years of wrongful living and wrongful thinking can lead a person to wrongful speaking. When words of this sort are expressed in private or in small circles, the damage is minimal, but when a wrongful activist places these words in a book for millions to read, the act becomes hugely offensive.

The Wrongful Activist will promote policies and behavior that benefit one group while causing pain to another. This lack of compassion for the sake of self-interest is a common trait of the Wrongful Activist and can be transferred to whole groups of followers who are easily manipulated. In September 2011, a question about health insurance was asked at a televised, political debate. The death of an innocent citizen was placed as a hypothetical scenario. Before the candidate could respond, a heckler from the audience yelled out a response that completely lacked compassion. It is a clear that this heckler is a product of a manipulating Wrongful Activist who promotes compassionless ideas.

3. Manipulates God and Religion for Wrongful Ends.

Historically, people have been manipulating God and religion to promote war, oppression, and other deplorable acts. During the nineteenth century, in the years leading to the US Civil War, southern pastors justified the institution of slavery on biblical grounds. Their followers were led to believe slavery was sanctioned by God. We now understand slavery to be wrong, but in those days Wrongful Activist found a way of manipulating people's religious beliefs for the benefit of a system that was inherently wrong. During the years leading to the civil rights movement,

God and Bible were often used to justify a stance. Bigotry held on to an interpretation of the Bible that justified segregation and institutionalized poverty. Civil rights activists held tightly to Gospel passages that prepared them for the confrontations that followed. Observers had to decide which side was manipulating God for wrongful ends. The Wrongful Activist of those days incited violence that, in many instances, not only caused pain and property damage but the death of innocent people. Eventually, enough people were able to realize that legalized bigotry is wrong and goodness prevailed. If we listen to the words of the Rev. Dr. Martin Luther King Jr., we clearly hear that his form of activism was spiritual and right because his language was nonviolent, leading people to positive and compassionate behavior. Dr. King is one of the leading role models for Spiritual Activists everywhere.

The Wrongful Activist will attempt to confuse her followers by citing God and the Bible. Listeners must examine carefully and have good discernment skills to separate the Wrongful Activist from the Spiritual Activist. A good example of this conflict is in the recent tug of war surrounding the issue of gay marriage. In many religious circles, the gay, lesbian, bisexual, and transgender (GLBT) community has been demonized. Wrongful Activists are claiming God hates gays in order to justify policies that keep the GLBT community oppressed. Likewise, the GLBT community is holding on to theological statements that God loves them as they are. The silent observer of this conflict may become confused. Which side is right? After all, they both claim God to justify their argument. The answer lies in examining the goal of the activist. If the goal is to keep people from expressing a human right that others enjoy, it is wrong. If the goal is to promote fear and divisions that perpetuates discord, it is wrong. If the goal will cause harm in any way, it is wrong. Such are the marks of the Wrongful Activist.

The Time for Spiritual Activism Is Now

The damage done to activism by religious institutions has led many progressive movements to exclude people of faith from the dialogue. Too many conservative and fundamentalist Christians and followers of television evangelists and the religious right have become involved in political campaigns that defend big corporations and the status quo. Consequently, an entire generation of activists is suspicious of Christians and would rather not work with them. These activists do not stop to consider that there are progressive people of faith who can be an asset to their movement. From their point of view, religious people are homophobic, sexist, and obstacles to change. Many have sound arguments to justify this stance. It is time to prove them wrong. It is time for progressive people of faith to stand up and be counted. It is time for an activist movement that is a response to God's call for justice. It is time for the rise of the Spiritual Activists.

Interview: Integrity, the Pathway to Activism

If I seem to take part in politics, it is only because politics
encircles us today like the coil of a snake from
which one cannot get out, no matter how much one tries.
I wish therefore to wrestle with the snake.

~Mohandas Gandhi

South Florida is the perfect setting for exploitation. Vulnerable people immigrate to Miami daily. They arrive mostly from South America and the Caribbean, with the hope of a better life. They arrive with little if any knowledge of the English language, the laws of the nation, and the resources available to them. Their vulnerability makes them the perfect candidates for exploitation. To think only immigrants are exploited in South Florida is delusional; many citizens of this fair nation fall prey to promises of employment, only to become victims of wage theft.

Jeanette Smith is a cheerful woman who laughs easily. Her welcoming smile is a genuine reflection of an inner happiness that flows freely. She has an abundance of energy, most likely fueled by her sense of purpose. She labors, speaks, and multitasks as if time were working against her.

For nearly two decades Jeanette has been one of the few people in South Florida to work for the labor and human rights of others. She worked for many years with the National Farm Worker Ministry, advocating for the rights of migrant farm workers in Florida, and currently is executive director of South Florida Interfaith Worker Justice, as well as an active member of the Friends Meeting House. Jeanette identifies herself as Quaker, an often-misunderstood religion.

Although the Quaker religion has deep Christian roots, it is not Christian. It was formed during an intentional separation from the institution of the Christian church in seventeenth-century England. Following the teachings of George Fox, a seventeenth-century religious activist, the Quaker religion deliberately avoids organizational structure and hierarchy. Quakers do not practice the Christian sacraments, nor do they believe in many of the Christians doctrines. They do not have a creed, but they do have five basic tenets, or testimonies: simplicity, integrity, equality, community, and peace.

Jeanette and I met at a local coffee shop for our conversation. She greeted me with her radiant smile and we laughed about small things. Although I have known Jeanette for several years and we share an important victory—helping the janitors at the University of Miami fight for fair labor rights—I knew very little about her origins. I always figured she was a northerner who somehow found her way to Miami. It turns out I was right.

Jeanette: I'm from Pennsylvania. I came to Miami a month shy of my twenty-first birthday.

Guillermo: And you stayed.

Jeanette [*laughing*]: I stayed. Back then I remember seeing that popular bumper sticker, "Will the last American leaving Miami please turn off the lights and bring home the flag?" And I thought to myself, who would want to leave this place? . . . I thought Miami was a wonderful, diverse mix.

Guillermo: And what brought you here a month shy of your twenty-first birthday?

Jeanette: School. I came to study international relations in Latin America and the Caribbean at FIU (Florida International University). That spring I came to visit and everyone I encountered was from somewhere else. You can't get that international feel anywhere. When you want to get an international degree, it's great to be in a place where there are so many people from everywhere.

Guillermo: You have several academic degrees, right?

Jeanette: Well, as I said, I have a bachelor's in international relations from FIU. I have a law degree . . . I also have a legal education certificate from the University of the West Indies so I can practice law over in the West Indies. I have a master's in comparative sociology and I'm finishing a PhD in social cultural anthropology.

Guillermo: Impressive.

Jeanette [*laughing*]: I am definitely over-educated.

Guillermo: Most over achievers are. So, tell me, you're a Quaker. (*Jeannette nods while sipping her tea.*) Were you born a Quaker?

Jeanette: No. I was baptized Catholic, although my family didn't go to church. My grandmother was half Native American, and I spent a lot of time with her. It wasn't until college that I started to go to the Catholic church . . . . And then I applied for a job with the American Friends Service Committee . . . they had given me a booklet on Quakerism . . . . Like the Rastafarians, Quakers don't like the "ism" [*laughs*] 'cause it puts them on the level of all the other "isms." Anyway, I went to their worship and realized I'm Quaker. I just am. I don't believe we convert to things. We just come to the realization of what we are.

Guillermo: The Quaker religion is not Christian.

Jeanette: No, it isn't. And I want to be clear about that. If you ask five Quakers, you might get three different answers [*laughs*]. Historically, it used to be Catholics, Protestants, and Quakers. The way we worship is not what others define as Christian. We do read the Bible, but we don't stop there. We're not Christo-centric, for lack of a better word. We look at the historical Jesus and the spiritual Jesus. A big difference is that we don't proselytize. If we are to not be, then we won't be. We don't seek to perpetuate ourselves. And that is not how Christianity works. Most churches spend a lot of time and money trying to get new people through the doors. We don't worry about that.

Guillermo: I'm going to make a statement and you can either affirm it or deny it, but there is a stereotype of Quakers as being justice oriented. Quakers integrate justice into their faith and life. What do you say to that?

Jeanette: Yes, we are, and yes, we do. It has to do with our testimonies . . . . We have five testimonies: simplicity, integrity, equality, community, and peace. How these testimonies manifest in our lives varies from person to person. They're guidelines, I suppose. Simplicity goes well with environmental issues, and for many Quakers it's, "Walk gently upon the earth." Integrity is more than truth, it is a continual awareness of who we are called to be. Peace, to quote Dr. Martin Luther King, is more than just the absence of tension—it is the presence of justice. Equality is the idea of everyone being equal and having a direct relationship with the spirit. So other faiths are equally valid.

In my case, there are so many other things I can be doing with my life that would be far more lucrative and where I would get a lot more rest. But this is my calling. And people ask me why I labor so hard for something that is so . . . Guillermo, I have to tell you I don't know how to stop doing what I do. This is my calling, my passion. So, for the most part, Quakers feel very strongly about their calling, whether it's the environment, or peace and nonviolence, or issues of immigration.

It's interesting that I've had conversations with people who identify themselves as atheists and I describe to them my Quaker faith and they respond, "Wait, maybe I'm Quaker" [*laughing*]. I hear that a lot: "Maybe I'm Quaker."

Guillermo: I was just thinking it too. Maybe I'm Quaker.

Jeanette [*laughs*]: Well, because it's natural.

Guillermo: Jeannette, you've been part of many justice efforts and campaigns. Can you talk to me about one that is particularly close to your heart?

Jeanette: Wage theft. Well, there've been a lot of things I've worked on: farm worker ministry, immigration, labor issues, the Justice for Janitors, but wage theft is something I've been working on for a long time.

Guillermo: What is wage theft?

Jeanette: Wage theft is one of several scenarios. The most egregious form of wage theft is for a worker to not get paid at all. Another form is to have wages withheld, which is very common, or to not get paid the agreed upon rate, or to not get paid the overtime. Wage theft might be not paying the taxes or the Social Security taxes or the agreed-upon benefits. The most egregious form of wage theft, that of not being paid at all, happens to the most vulnerable like illegal immigrants or sometimes legal citizens who are trapped into the system and stay with it in hopes of getting paid sometime in the future. The employer says, "I can't pay you this week, but I promise I'll pay you next week." And the worker returns because she has no other place to work, but most importantly because she's owed money.

It's almost like indentured servitude. A man called me this morning . . . Heath works in the construction industry. He told me, "I worked for them for three years and I never got my full pay. I would get one hundred fifty dollars one week, and they would tell me I would get the rest at the end of the month, but then at the end of the month they would be two hundred dollars short." So they kept Heath chained to the job with the hope of getting his full pay one day. The money just kind of dribbled along and he never saw a full paycheck. In the meantime, Heath has to pay his electric bill, his rent. Now how can anyone plan a budget under those circumstances? How can anyone plan to move ahead in life if you never know what you're going to be paid?

Guillermo: Shouldn't this be unlawful?

Jeanette: It is unlawful, but in many cases it's very difficult to enforce. When we started to look into wage theft, we were amazed as to how prevalent it is. We spoke to the attorney general, and there was no local ordinance in the state of Florida. So we set out to write the ordinance. And [laughs] we wrote it [laughs harder]. We actually wrote it.

Guillermo: Well, that's why we collaborate with each other. Call it "teamwork."

Jeanette: Yes, let's call it that . . . . The ordinance was passed in February of 2010 and it is the first of its kind in the state and in the country. November 2010 was when the implementing order was passed, which is what's needed after the ordinance is accepted. November 16—the Board of County Commissioners at our urging also declared it "Day against Wage Theft."

And then wage theft claims started coming right away, even before the ordinance was implemented. Wage theft claims were processed through the Wage Theft Program administered through the Small Business Development. That department was chosen for several reasons, but most importantly is that wage theft is more than just about the employees who are not being paid. It's also about businesses. It's bad for business growth because a bad employer can undercut another by turning in lower bids for contracts. He can do that because he knows he's not going to pay his workers. Also, when people don't get paid they don't have the income to purchase other goods and stimulate the economy.

Guillermo: Let's back up a little. What work did you have to do in order to pass the ordinance and have it implemented?

Jeanette: Well, we had to put together the Wage Theft Task Force. It represented a broad community collaboration between the faith community, labor, worker's rights groups, researchers, and public interest attorneys and some business groups.

Guillermo: How many people were in this task force?

Jeanette: The organizations represented were thirteen. At one point it went up to twenty, and then there were peripheral members. We had to choose a county commissioner (Natacha Seijas). She is a Republican, which was nice because wage theft is not a partisan issue. We also had many volunteers from the faith community. They did most of the phone calls.

Guillermo: So what does the ordinance ask for?

Jeanette: The ordinance is designed to help the low-wage earner petition monies that are due to him or her. Workers can file a claim for as low as sixty dollars because usually the people who get cheated most often are domestic and day laborers, who labor from day to day for the promise of making seventy-five or a hundred dollars and then only get paid a portion. If the ordinance required a higher claim like two hundred fifty dollars, then it would eliminate the people who get cheated the most. There's no cost to file a claim. The idea is to make it accessible and reasonably quick.

One challenge we've had is the flood of claims. The county has been overwhelmed with claims. To date they've managed to bring about $365,000 for 244 workers and an additional $400,000 in claims that have gone to court. Yet, there's another $1.7 million in claims that have yet to be processed, and the calls keep coming in every week.

Guillermo: It's eye-opening to think South Florida has so much wage theft!

Jeanette: It's horrible! I want to point out to you something that is important to understand. It is heart-wrenching to hear how a worker is humiliated by having to beg for pay that is owed her. Someone has worked and earned her wages and feels that she has to justify her pay because her rent is due, her bills are due, or she can't buy Pampers for her baby. It is so humiliating!

No one should ever have to justify getting paid for work he has done. If people got to see how workers have to beg, wage theft would not be tolerated. And this is not an issue of undocumented workers, or legal versus illegal workers. This is across the board. This is a very equal-opportunity injustice. The more marginalized tend to be the more vulnerable. Women are most vulnerable, and too often they work longer hours than the men for less pay. The Miami-Dade Women's Fund did a study on women's economic security in Miami and found that a lot of women have suffered wage theft. These women are law-abiding citizens, people who pay taxes.

Although the emotional argument is very strong, there are economic arguments as to why wage theft is bad. It's not anti-capitalism. I get people who are suspicious of this ordinance and they look at me as if I were a socialist, which doesn't bother me [*laughs*]. But people need to understand that a basic principle of the capitalist system is to pay your employees. When people are paid for the work they do, they can participate in the broader economy and they can help raise children that will do the same.

Guillermo: How long did it take for this ordinance to pass? I'm talking about from the moment you dreamed about it to when it became a reality.

Jeanette: Almost two years. We began this process in 2008, when a group of day laborers were being physically abused and mistreated by an employer. So at that time, a group of us were looking at this problem and we realized that it reached beyond this particular mistreatment. Yeah, it took a while, almost two years, because we had to do a lot of research. Once we passed it we entered a new phase, and that was of defending the ordinance.

Guillermo: Will the current political climate help or hinder the ordinance?

Jeanette: Right now, there's an effort to undermine it. We're getting some push back from the American Retail Federation, which is distressing to me. There's a bill at the state level from the Florida Retail Federation. Senator Simmons from Orange County and Representative Goodson from Titusville have submitted matching bills in the House and Senate to preempt it. The Florida Retail Federation is pushing it and the Association of Builders and Contractors is supporting it.

Guillermo: What is this bill called?

Jeanette: Wage Theft Employee Protection Act—something like that.

Guillermo: It sounds like it would benefit the employees.

Jeanette: It sounds great, but it's really a misnomer. The bill is very short. It's only five lines and it argues that wage theft is already handled at the federal and state levels;

therefore, the counties should not be doing this. Any effort to address this at the county level should be struck down. That's it. It's very simple.

Guillermo: What is their argument for presenting this bill?

Jeanette: Well, let me see . . . . This is an issue for the big companies that have stores across the state. It's not that they are saying wage theft is good or legal. What they're saying is that if every county writes its own ordinance, it becomes a legal nightmare for them. They don't want to have stores across the state and have to figure out what the rules are for this county and for that county and so forth. If you're building homes across the state you don't want to deal with sixty-seven different wage theft laws. So, in essence they're pushing for the statewide system to regulate wage theft. This is a push for bigger government at the state level.

Guillermo: What do you say to that?

Jeanette: Several things. First, pay your employees and this won't even be a concern for you. Second, the larger businesses like Publix (supermarket) and other large employers would not fall under the jurisdiction of our wage theft ordinance because they fall under the Wage and Hour Division of the federal government. So they shouldn't even be in this conversation. They don't have a dog in this fight, or a horse in this race, however you want to phrase it.

The wage theft ordinance is not creating a new regulation. The law is and has been that if you work you should get paid. That has already been codified and is the law. All the wage theft ordinance is doing is providing a venue for the claim to be handled in a more expeditious manner. If you move the enforcement to the state, which is where it was before, then it will make the program ineffective, especially for the low-wage earner. The people at the bottom of the economic ladder need something accessible and easy.

I tried explaining the ordinance to Rep. Tom Goodson from Titusville and he told me he didn't want to hear it. He said he doesn't want Miami-Dade telling him what to do. He's a contractor with work across the state.

Guillermo: He doesn't make any sense. Shall we call him "hear no evil"?

Jeanette: It's like he's proud of his ignorance and doesn't want to become informed. Some people tell me that if we start regulating the business sector, it's bad for jobs. Well, guess what? A job with no pay is not a job. If I can get people to have a conversation about it, and to read the ordinance, then people will see it's not socialism.

Guillermo: People are afraid of socialism. Let me change the subject. The world is in need of more people becoming active in issues of social justice. Where do you think we need more activists?

Jeanette: Well, there are a lot of problems. And our world is suffering from too many illnesses. I think most problems stem from a lack of respect. I think that if most people were treated with respect, we'd eliminate half the problems of our world. I don't want to discount work on the environment or on nonviolence. Quakers have a strong commitment to the nonviolent movement. But I do think that when people cannot take care of their basic needs—a roof over their heads, food for their children—everything else is undermined. They can't even think beyond survival. It's like Maslow's Hierarchy of Needs. First provide the basics before I can go deeper into other matters. If we can't take care of those things at the bottom of the pyramid, people can't move up.

Wage theft and unemployment really hit this. When people work and get paid for their work, they are able to take care of their needs and move up the ladder to other areas of development, be it intellectual or spiritual.

Guillermo: So if you were going to speak to a future activist, an aspiring activist, what advice would you give that person?

Jeanette: I would say, "Know what you're passionate about. Interact with the people who are affected by the issue and find out what they think. There's a lot of work to be done but there's no reason to do it alone. Also, don't get overwhelmed with all the work." When I was a little girl, my grandmother used to tell me I can't change the world, but I can change my little corner of it. And I think that's true. It's very true. We may not like what's happening nationwide, but let's take a look at what's happening in our own backyards and strive to change what's wrong.

Jeanette and I parted wishing each other a happy holiday. Within steps of each other, she began to listen to her phone messages. I was reminded of the many duties she juggles daily.

I waved one last time, and she turned to me with a laugh. Her laughter resonated throughout the parking lot, and I thought, *There goes a genuinely joyful woman.*

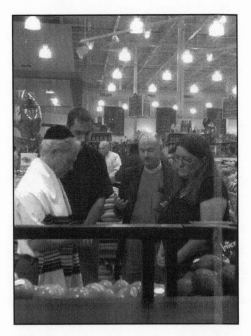

*Jeanette Smith in the midst of an inter-faith protest prayer
in Publix Supermarket (February, 2012)*

CHAPTER 3

The Trap of Well—Intentioned Wrongful Activism

Hell is full of good intentions or desires.

~Saint Bernard of Clairvaux

The study of ethics is concerned with the timeless question, "Does the end justify the means?" Because ethics is not a field of study in most secondary schools, many a young person enters adulthood not aware that the journey is more important than the goal. Too many people have only the goal in mind, and in their desperate rush for immediate gratification, they "do what they have to do" in order to reach their goal. Ethics states that how a person reaches the decision is more important than the decision itself. What are the factors considered in making the decision? Was the decision made for egotistical or altruistic reasons? Many people do not take the time to consider such factors because they haven't had training in the field of ethics. Consequently, many well-intentioned people have committed regrettable mistakes.

Activism, as a field, is vulnerable to unethical or immoral acts because some activists have ceased to think about their decision-making process. They believe the end justifies the means. They are incapable of considering their actions immoral because they are in pursuit of idealistic goals. Their sin is nestled in the moral dissonance in their rhetoric by committing one wrong while attempting to rectify another. Such activists may have begun as well-intentioned Spiritual Activists, but at some point in their journey they fell into the trap of wrongful activism.

When the pro-life/antiabortion movement began in 1973, the proponents did not consider that its rhetoric would contribute to acts of violence and killings ten years later. This rhetoric came under scrutiny after the bombing of several clinics and the death of (and injury to) doctors, nurses, and security guards. Several pro-life organizations, including Advocates for Life Ministries[7] promoted justifiable homicide in their effort to protect life. When pro-life activists were killing in the name of life, the moral dissonance was deafening. How did the words of the movement, be it official or unofficial, make it seem justifiable for followers to consider such violent thoughts? The lesson learned is that the principles of nonviolence need to be taught, promoted, and urged at all levels of the movement. This lesson can be witnessed in the intentional effort the pro-life movement has made in the last twenty years to deliver its message in nonviolent rhetoric.

Nonviolence is an integral part of all spiritual activism. Nonviolence requires strength and control, for it is often easy to yield to violence. Nonviolence reaches beyond good intentions and builds on the deliberate and intentional focus of creating positive change. For a Spiritual Activist to valiantly hold her ground in the adversarial face of violent, menacing forces is no easy task. It requires the right approach, the right focus, the right disposition, the right inner strength, and the right leadership. In the United States we have witnessed the power of nonviolence in the work of the Rev. Dr. Martin Luther King Jr. and the civil rights movement. In his 1966 speech "Nonviolence: The Only Road to Freedom," Dr. King explained the philosophy behind his nonviolent approach.[8]

> Our most powerful nonviolent weapon, as would be expected, also our most demanding, is organization. To produce change, people must be organized to work together in units of power . . . . The power of the nonviolent march is indeed a mystery . . . . When marches are carefully organized around well-defined issues, they represent the power, which Victor Hugo phrased as the most powerful force in the world, "An idea whose time has come." Marching feet announce that time has come for a given idea. When the idea is a sound one, the cause is a just one, and the demonstration a righteous one, change will be forthcoming . . . when marching is seen as a part of a program to dramatize an evil, to mobilize the forces of good will, and to generate pressure

and power for change, marches will continue to be effective.

[A]long with the march as a weapon for change in our nonviolent arsenal must be listed the boycott. Basic to the philosophy of nonviolence is the refusal to cooperate with evil. There is nothing quite so effective as a refusal to cooperate economically with the forces and institutions that perpetuate evil in our communities.

There is no easy way to create a world where men and women can live together, where each has his own job and house and where all children receive as much education as their minds can absorb. But if such a world is created in our lifetime, it will be done in the United States by Negroes and white people of good will. It will be accomplished by persons who have the courage to put an end to suffering by willingly suffering themselves rather than inflict suffering upon others. It will be done by rejecting the racism, materialism, and violence that has characterized Western civilization and especially by working toward a world of brotherhood, cooperation, and peace.

The trap of wrongful activism is easy to fall into when the activist is not trained in the principles of nonviolence. It is not the purpose of this book to substitute with a few pages of information what deserves deeper understanding. Yet, the principles of nonviolence[9] as lived and taught by the Rev. Dr. Martin Luther King Jr. and by Mohandas Gandhi need to be mentioned in the hopes of inspiring further study. For the novice inspired into activism, it is important to know these principles. In the long run, all justice efforts will be measured not by the goal they sought to reach, but by the path they chose to reach it.

Principles of Nonviolence

1. Nonviolence is a way of life for courageous people.

    a. It is active nonviolent resistance to wrongfulness.
    b. It is assertive spiritually, mentally, and emotionally.
    c. It is always persuading the opponent of the justice of the cause.

2. Nonviolence seeks to win friendships and understanding.

    a. The end result of nonviolence is redemption and reconciliation.
    b. The purpose of nonviolence is the creation of the [righteous] community.

3. Nonviolence seeks to defeat injustice, not people.

    a. Nonviolence holds that wrongdoers are victims too.

4. Nonviolence holds that voluntary suffering can educate and transform.

   a. Nonviolence willingly accepts the consequences of its acts.
   b. Nonviolence accepts suffering without retaliation.
   c. Nonviolence accepts violence, if necessary, but will never inflict it.
   d. Suffering can have the power to convert the enemy when reason fails.

5. Nonviolence chooses love over hate.

   a. Nonviolence resists violence of the spirit as well as of the body.
   b. Nonviolent love gives willingly, knowing that the return might be hostility.
   c. Nonviolent love is active, not passive.
   d. Nonviolent love does not sink to the level of the hater.
   e. Love for the enemy is how we demonstrate love for ourselves.
   f. Love restores community and resists injustice.
   g. Nonviolence recognizes that all life is interrelated.

6. Nonviolence believes the universe is on the side of justice.

   a. Justice will always prevail.
   b. Nonviolence believes that God is a God of justice.

Nonviolence is a spiritual practice that runs counter to the corporate inclination of fighting, especially when people are gathered in large groups promoting an atmosphere of violence. Walter Wink, in his book *Engaging the Powers*, wrote about the "demons" that are living inside every person and become manifest in collective situations. He used the analogy of a riot at a soccer match. What power possessed the fans at a soccer match that led them to riot? Did the "riot demon" overcome them, or was it a "wrongful spirituality" that crystallized when triggered by the violent ethos of the game, the heavy drinking, and the inner violence of the fans? Many of these rioters are individuals who, in any other situation, would try to resolve a conflict peacefully. Yet in the frenzy of the moment, they convince each other to riot.

The Spiritual Activist needs to recognize that the same frenzy possessing fans at a soccer match can be promoted by Wrongful Activists, leading entire communities to embrace a violent ethos. Human systems have been built to allow in the corporate what the individual would not dare: to dominate others into submission. Consequently, the evil in systems of domination is what nonviolence seeks to counter. Nonviolence provides a new model of interrelations between people and communities. Nonviolence promotes a spirit of redemption to allow for peace to be a tangible, breathable presence in the community.

Too often people mistake the stillness created by oppressive dominating forces as peace. If I have my foot on the throat of another human being, and I force that person to submit, I have not achieved peace. I have created a moment of stillness created by domination. Wink uses the term "domination system" to describe an organized force that seeks to dominate others by any means available. A domination system can be organized crime in the form of a street gang or mafia. It can also be an entire nation or a militarized subunit of the nation. To fight a domination system with violence is to replace one evil with another, one domination with another. True peace is the outcome of a nonviolent process of reconciliation and dialogue. The world has witnessed the success of nonviolence in the struggles of India, South Africa, and the civil rights movement, providing a model for the world to follow. Sadly, too many systems of domination are following an ethos of fear, thinking that only through domination of "the other" will peace become a reality. In such systems, peace can never be achieved, for violence begets more violence. The domination system fools itself in thinking, "If only I could get stronger by acquiring more weapons and soldiers, then I could win and peace will follow." The Spiritual Activist knows such thoughts are delusional.

Consider the Israel/Palestine conflict as a failed example of a domination system.[10] The Israeli government seeks to dominate the Palestinian people through force. Although the Palestinian people have been choked by the very muscular Israeli army, peace is not at hand. Should the Palestinians continue to choose violence as a response to the military presence that is choking them, they will lose more lives and continue to feed the vicious cycle of violence.

Fortunately, a nonviolent movement is arising from the ashes. Following the model created by the South African Truth and Reconciliation Commission, Israeli and Palestinian activists from the Christian, Jewish, and Muslim communities are working together in nonviolent means of protest to overcome the domination system that created and sustains the conflict.[11]

Consider the war between the United States and Afghanistan as another failed example of domination systems. Our continued military presence in Afghanistan is no longer our response to the 9/11 attacks and terror. Osama bin Laden has been killed. The forces of Al-Qaeda have been identified to be residing in other parts of the world. Anti-terror strategies are in place to neutralize and weaken those forces, which are no longer in Afghanistan. So what exactly is the United States trying to achieve with a continued military presence that is promoting violence? In seeking to dominate Afghanistan and its people into submission, we are engaged in a war we cannot win. The continued flexing of military muscles in Afghanistan raises several questions for the Spiritual Activist to consider. Does our military presence in Afghanistan promote the democratic values of our nation? Are we betraying our constitutional principles with our imperialistic need to dominate the Afghan people? As Spiritual Activists we must stand for peace and resist the culture of domination that is permeating the ethos of the United States.

As Spiritual Activists we recognize that all life is interrelated, motivating us to seek peace through nonviolence. We tackle the systems of domination, be they domestic or foreign, through nonviolent means. Nonviolence defeats injustice, not people. It seeks to engage people, including our perceived enemy, in finding a nonviolent solution. Knowing that only the power of love can restore, we must organize and train communities to respond to violence through nonviolence. Most importantly, Spiritual

Activists must be aware of the evil embedded within the governing structure and unite voters and citizens to direct their attention to it. Only through the power of unified, nonviolent citizens can the dominating powers be moved to change.

Nonviolence is not easy. It requires training and the support of a nonviolent community. Not everyone can practice it, but everyone should try. The challenge of nonviolence is that it runs counter to the message of the society created by a dominating system. Societies of domination promote an image of the strong that is rooted in violence. The hero is the person who can fight and has muscular fortitude. Societies of domination do not promote a hero who is peaceful or whose fortitude is rooted in faith. Yet if we consider Desmond Tutu, Mohandas Gandhi, and Martin Luther King Jr., men who led a nonviolent revolution that defeated the systems of domination, we will understand a different kind of strength. Gandhi said that nonviolence is the weapon of the strong. It is an instrument of choice wielded with deliberation. It is the victory of principles and conviction over impulse and anger. Nonviolence is the way for long-lasting change. It is the way of the Spiritual Activist.

CHAPTER 4

Capitalism Is Not a Spiritual Practice, Simplicity Is

Modern capitalism needs men who cooperate smoothly and in large numbers; who want to consume more and more; and whose tastes are standardized and can be easily influenced and anticipated . . . what is the outcome? Modern man is alienated from himself, from his fellow man, and from nature.

~Erich Fromm, *Wisdom for the Soul*

Every weekday morning the local news channel has a beautiful, at times sexy, reporter giving the weather report. We may not be able to control the weather, but we certainly are fascinated by it, especially when an attractive young person is on the screen providing a narration about the different pressure systems coming our way. Minutes later another beautiful reporter is standing on the floor of the New York Stock Exchange ready to give the financial report. Similar in style to the weather report, the market report alerts the audience to the different economic waves coming our way.

The unintended effect for the audience is the sense that we have no control over either system. Tornadoes may emerge out of nowhere and stock prices may plummet, and the average citizen is helpless to effect either. Although this may be true, there is a huge difference. The market is not a natural phenomenon. The economy is not created by the earth's rotation or by solar flares. The economy is a human invention. We may not have any ability to control the rainstorms forming around us, but we can certainly influence the economy. We don't make rain, but we do make the economy; therefore, we have more power to influence the economy than we may believe. Spiritual Activists must understand basic economic principles in order to understand the best approach for injecting change into such a large system.

More importantly, we must stop attributing virtues to capitalism that are not inherent to it. Too many Wrongful Activists have been upholding capitalism as the cornerstone of our democracy and of a virtuous system that needs to be left alone. Many scholars argue that capitalism needs to be regulated in order for all members of society to benefit. Regulation, however, is fought by those who do not want their earnings kept in check. They spend time and money promoting a rhetoric that ascribes capitalism to the virtuous thoughts of the nation's Founding Fathers and wrongfully attack critics as unpatriotic socialists. It seems that these defenders of modern capitalism forget that it was the unfair economic policies, as well as the gross economic inequality in eighteenth-century Europe that led to the revolutionary words and actions of our Founding Fathers.

How far government reaches into the market system to regulate is a continual subject of discussion. In 1776, British economist and philosopher Adam Smith wrote the landmark book *The Wealth of Nations*, still considered required reading in the field of classical economics. While Smith lived in a monarchical country that favored the ultra-rich, his words still ring true two centuries later as wealth is increasingly accumulated in the pockets of a select circle of privileged people. He wrote, "Civil government, so far as it is instituted for the security of property, is in reality instituted for the defense of the rich against the poor, or of those who have some property against those who have none at all . . . . It is not very unreasonable that the rich should contribute to the public expense, not only in proportion to their revenue, but something more than in that proportion."

The Insidious Corruption of Capitalism

The nineteenth century was a time of political upheaval throughout most of Europe. The paradigms were shifting from monarchies to democracies. The economies were moving from agricultural to industrial, local to global. As the political and economic landscape changed, opportunities emerged for new businesses and new sources of revenue. However, these opportunities were only available to those people with means and access to the resources at hand. In European countries that did not entirely undo the monarchical system, the competition was unfair and unbalanced. Lords with royal titles inherited huge tracts of land from the monarchy and then plundered it for their gain. With a considerable wealth already in existence, they entered the capitalist race with a significant head start, ensuring their place at the top of the economic ladder. Middle-class people, hoping to enter this race, had a significant disadvantage, making it nearly impossible for them to catch up to the privileged aristocratic circles.

The United States had the promise of a non-monarchical system in which everyone could enter the race from the same starting line. It was a wonderful experiment that promised to provide opportunity for many, not just the few. But even in this land of opportunity there was inequality built into the system from the very beginning, turning a beautiful ideal into another field of oppression. Many Southern plantations grew their wealth on the backs of African American slaves. Many women were forbidden from entering the business sector, keeping them in poverty or in unhealthy marriages. Land was stolen from the Native Americans and distributed to members of elite inner circles for the mining of copper, gold, and silver. Sadly, the promises of capitalism to provide upward mobility to many were distorted to benefit the few. It is crucial that a Spiritual Activist be aware of this history and look beyond the fabled, romantic versions presented. Only in a balanced and fair view of history can an explanation be found for the collective pain of entire communities.

History is a multifaceted subject that is often told in a lopsided manner. For far too many generations, American history was written by the dominant Anglo culture that was in love with itself. The voices of the African American, the Native American, and other oppressed groups were kept out of the story. In the last twenty-five years a more balanced approach to historical research has been emerging. Scholars have provided a new storyline that shows how the business interests of a few men shaped the policies and the social structure of the nineteenth century. If you read carefully, removing the romanticized images, the US narrative of westward expansion is littered with greed, murder, genocide, and the abuse of God's creation. One hundred years later, whole communities were enjoying the benefits of those nineteenth-century policies, yet many others were living in poverty and oppression so the dominant culture could prosper. If you doubt the truth of this statement, speak to the descendants of the Black Foot tribe in Wyoming. Speak to the descendants of African Americans slaves or to Latina or Middle Eastern women who have been pushed down repeatedly by a dominant culture that prefers to see them as servants. A spiritual activist cannot be blinded by a romantic version of history that sweeps the pain of whole communities under the rug.

While in the pursuit of the reparations for America's discriminatory past, too many people were blamed for the sins of their ancestors. The dominant Anglo community has for the last sixty years been receiving a barrage of angry rhetoric from angry minorities that at times seems hateful and destructive. To their credit, many Anglo people have sought to undo the wrongs that were committed. To their credit, many a wealthy family has fought to change the inequities of the system so others can prosper. The Carnegie, Kennedy, Roosevelt, Gates, and Buffet families, along with many others, have provided examples as to how wealthy people can create positive change and fight to undo systemic injustice. Yet generations later, many minority groups are still stuck in unending cycles of poverty. Why?

One factor we must consider is the insidious nature of capitalism. Capitalism is generally understood as an economic system in which the means of production are privately owned and operated for profit, usually in competitive markets. As an economic system of trade, it has no moral code. The ethical boundaries of any capitalistic system must be created by an ethical government. In order for the system to work ethically there must be a clear divide between the private and public sectors, allowing for government to regulate the corporate and financial sectors for the good of the whole community. Sadly, the boundaries between the private and public sectors have become blurred. Consequently, regulations that protect the environment and laborers have been loosened for the sake of corporate profits.

Noam Chomsky, in his book *Profit over People*, explains that the current neoliberal economic paradigm keeps control of the political process in the hands of a few private interests. Neoliberalism has paved the path for a corporate domination of society. Chomsky bluntly states that "eloquent proponents of neoliberalism sound as if they are doing poor people, the environment, and everybody else a tremendous service as they enact policies on behalf of the wealthy few."[12]

A Spiritual Activist must remember that the driving force in capitalism is the acquisition of money and assets, not the welfare of the people. It is a simple "sink or swim" economic model. Economists like Adam Smith have called for a distinct separation between the public and private sector, or else the entire system will be subject to corruption. With such noble minds leading the way it must be asked, "How did such a promising concept like capitalism become so corrupted so quickly?" The answer lies in the greed of the human heart.

Almost two millennia ago, the author of the Pauline Epistle to Timothy wrote that "the love of money is the root of all sorts of evil . . ." About eighteen hundred years later, author Louisa May Alcott paraphrased the words of the apostle and wrote, "Money is the root of all evil." Both authors lived in a society that did not have the complicated economic problems we have today, yet they were able to see that human greed is most visible when addressing issues of money. Mohandas Gandhi wrote that "capital as such is not evil. The evil is its wrong use . . ." I offer that to deregulate capitalism is the sin of greed.

Economic justice is a field concerned with the economic issues that create and perpetuate inequality. A Spiritual Activist needs to be prepared to enter the most damaging tension in society today: the gross economic inequality that is perpetuated by fiscal policies that benefit corporations and the wealthy. To enter this arena will most surely give rise to the Wrongful Activists who defend those injustices. It is at this point that a Spiritual Activist will wrongfully be accused of being a socialist. This accusation is as offensive to a Spiritual Activist as an accusation of being a capitalist. A Spiritual Activist is neither, nor does he promote a political party of any sort, for history has shown wrongful policies created by members from both side of the political aisle. A Spiritual Activist is to remain above the fray and should worry only about having the right understanding, right thought, right speech, right action, right livelihood, and right mindfulness.

Although it is obvious that I am highly critical of capitalism as it is currently practiced in the neoliberal paradigm, I have to state that socialism is not the answer either. Although I disapprove of the imperial, capitalistic nature of the United States, I am not promoting a socialist state. History has proven that socialist states do not work, for ultimately they restrict the basic human right of every individual to pursue his or her dreams. Failed socialist states such as Cuba, the Soviet Union, Czechoslovakia, and Vietnam are historical proof that governments will ultimately oppress the people they profess to care for. The sociopolitical experiment of socialism is proven to not work. And within the next few decades, the neoliberal model of capitalism will also be proven to not work. But because capitalism is still held as a savior, or as an American core value that must not be regulated or criticized, I must continue to address how it is the cause of erosion to society and to the human soul.

In the fall of 2011, one-time Republican presidential hopeful Herman Cain stated that to criticize the basics of capitalism was un-American.[13] So the question must be raised, "Does questioning capitalism jeopardize the foundation of this nation?" People unfamiliar with the US constitution might be surprised to learn that capitalism is not a listed constitutional right. For the people who defend capitalism as a virtuous economic system, we must remind them that capitalism is not a spiritual practice.

Those Wrongful Activists who want to deregulate capitalism and promote it as the vision of the Founding Fathers are feeding the people a lie for the sole benefit of corporations and the wealthy. Many people believe this lie and defend it with the passion of someone who is defending his home against an invader. Because one lie demands another, the lies needed to justify capitalism have gotten too large and the contradictions too blatant. Thankfully, a new awareness is emerging. People who normally were unaware of any problems are now asking new questions: Why is the gap between the rich and the poor getting larger? What is it about our capitalistic system that is creating a permanent underclass and a super upper class? What specifically about our economic and financial system is unfair? These questions are important and need to be explored. No one answer may be sufficient, but to reach a deeper understanding, let us consider an analogy between the neoliberal capitalistic system and a family suffering with an addiction.

Capitalism in the United States: An Unregulated Addiction

Consider the Smith family living in any metropolitan US city. Ma and Pa Smith are both addicted to gambling. They gamble at the casino, on the horse races, as well as on the Lotto jackpot. The Smiths get a rush every time they win, which is not as often as the times they lose. Nevertheless, they are addicted to that sensation. While fully aware that "the house always wins," they cannot help themselves. They must place a bet, even though the chances of losing are high. They are ill and in need of professional help. With regularity they visit a "shady" character to place bets on sports games. When they lose and don't pay, the "shady" character threatens their livelihood. Consequently, they often have to sell their car, jewels, and other assets.

The Smiths' children are growing up in this addictive environment, learning at an early age the "art" of gambling and beginning to imitate their parents' gambling behavior. One of their sons realizes in his early teens, when his father loses the rent money at the horse races, that something is terribly wrong. The son recognizes that there is a madness embedded in his parents' outlook on life. He knows this madness needs to stop, and he plans to do something about it.

He approaches the "shady" character and asks him to no longer accept his father's money. The "shady" character says, "Sorry, kid. Your father owes me too much money." He begs the casino and racetrack employees not to allow his parents in, but they just laugh at him. It doesn't take long for the boy to figure out that these establishments depend on his parents' gambling. If they stop gambling, these businesses would lose money. They are part of the problem. Consequently, there can only be one solution: stop the madness by eliminating the gambling source.

American consumerism is diseased in the same manner as the Smith family. A vicious cycle has been created among the banks, the corporations, and the consumers. This cycle is fueled by consumers spending their money. If people don't buy stuff, then the economic engine slows down. Consequently, every effort is made to increase the spending pattern of the people. The more people spend, the more money is injected into the economy, yielding higher profit rates for corporations. When consumers don't have money to spend, they are encouraged to acquire a credit card even when their household income cannot sustain more debt. Just in case consumers may listen to their common sense and slow down their spending, advertising firms are hired to create the illusion of needing the latest fashions, gadgets, and appliances. The corporations don't care how this spending negatively affects the families, for their main concern is to make a profit. Regardless of how much entire communities may be suffering, the message is to go out and spend.

The most egregious example of this is in the message from President George W. Bush after the country was attacked by terrorists on September 11, 2001. Instead of asking people to spend time with their loved ones, the president asked the nation to participate in the economy and spend money.[14] People were afraid of being bombed and terrorized, but we were asked to go shopping. Why? The answer lies in the analogy of the Smith family and to admit that society is ill. Richard Foster claims that to conform to a sick society is to be sick.[15]

The 9/11 tragedy was a missed opportunity to make significant changes in how America consumes and disposes of resources, and we cannot wait for another tragedy to address the ethical dilemma we are facing. Every citizen and resident must examine his or her spending pattern and ask, "Do I continue to feed this system by perpetuating my debt, or do I seek to stop the madness?"

The best way a Spiritual Activist can stop the madness is to embrace simplicity. I am reminded of the Native American proverb, "Live simply so that others may simply live." This adage recognizes that everything acquired is always at the expense of someone else. It is common sense to many people, but for the sake of proving the argument, consider the following formula for an average consumer living in an average city. x = the amount of goods and property owned and y = the amount of resources required to fuel and care for x

If x = y, then 10x = 10y and 100x =100y

This formula does not reflect a problem as long as both variables are limitless. In a world of limitless resources, there are no concerns. Y can increase at the same rate as x and it will not matter. The problem is that everyone knows we live in a world where resources are limited. Time, budget, and environmental resources are limited. Consequently, x should increase only at a rate that does not deplete y. However, that is not reality. In households with a debt and consumerism problem, the formula looks more like x=2y, x=4y, or worse. Few households develop the inverse formula, such as 2x = y, 4x = y, or better.

In today's world, where the message is to buy, spend, and acquire, the discipline of simplicity is more important than ever. The economic system requires consumers to be in constant debt. For centuries, the word "debt" has always had a negative connotation, and for good reasons. Debt is a form of bondage. The more a person owes, the more the person has to work to pay the debt. The more the person has to work, the less time she has to enjoy the simple things of life. People in debt are not free to use their money as they please. Yet the economic system promotes debt by enticing consumers to apply for more credit cards so they can spend more. Eventually, many consumers spend more than they earn and find themselves afloat in a sea of debt. Then they have to work not for self-fulfillment or enjoyment but because they are obligated to pay off their debt.

So how does a consumer stop the madness and become free from such bondage? Embrace simplicity and subtract wants and needs from your life. Meister Eckhart said that "the spiritual life has more to do with subtraction than with addition." [16] The person who embraces simplicity is free to dedicate her money to more humane activity as opposed to paying off debt. In the words of Richard Foster, "Simplicity is freedom."[17] The person who embraces simplicity will not have to work overtime and has more time to dedicate to loved ones. The person who embraces simplicity can dedicate more time to a prayerful life and to spiritual disciplines instead of having to work long hours to pay off debt. Simplicity not only makes good economic sense, it promotes a healthy perspective in a world that is ill with consumerism.

The Wrongful Activist will promote consumerism, not for the benefit of the individual but for the benefit of the economic system. The Spiritual Activist will promote simplicity for the benefit of the individual and the community. Simplicity calls for people to reduce the need for consumption in order to reduce the amount of resources consumed. In environmental circles this is called "reducing your carbon footprint." Simplicity goes beyond the carbon footprint and calls for all aspects of daily life to be reduced. The most powerful statement a Spiritual Activist can make is to reduce the amount of debt incurred and the number of credit cards owned. For the Smith family, the only way to stop the madness of gambling is to stop gambling. Likewise for people everywhere, the way to stop the madness of an economic system that perpetuates debt is to live simply.

To embrace simplicity is to also claim time. Simplify and your time will be yours—not your boss's. Simplify and the pressure to be constantly moving is eliminated. Simplify and there will be time to stop and enjoy every moment. Consider the number of people you know who complain they don't have enough time for life's basic pleasures. Consider the number of people who spend too much time in traffic, or working overtime to make ends meet, or rushing around all day from needless activity to needless activity.

A century ago, the poet W. H. Davies wrote the following:

> *What is this life if, full of care, we have no time to*
> *stand and stare?*
> *No time to stand beneath the boughs and stare as*
> *long as sheep or cows.*
> *No time to see, when woods we pass, where squirrels*
> *hide their nuts in grass.*
> *No time to see, in broad daylight, streams full of*
> *stars, like skies at night.*
> *No time to turn at Beauty's glance, and watch her*
> *feet, how they can dance.*
> *No time to wait till her mouth can enrich that smile*
> *her eyes began.*
> *A poor life this is if, full of care, we have no time to*
> *stand and stare.*[18]

It is a universal and timeless challenge to not allow the rhythm and desires of a consumer-oriented world to dictate our priorities. For centuries, poets and spiritual leaders have been promoting simplicity as the antidote to the poisonous lifestyle that contaminates the priorities of people. Embrace simplicity and regain your power over your economy, schedule and focus. Embrace simplicity and stop the madness.

Interview: Lifestyle as a Form of Activism

A man can live and be healthy without killing animals for food;
therefore, if he eats meat, he participates in taking animal life
merely for the sake of his appetite. And to act so is immoral.
~Leo Tolstoy, On Civil Disobedience

Noel and Carol have been a couple since the late '90s, when their common interests on the environment, vegan food, and justice provided the doorway for their romance. Noel is an engineer and a part-time musician. He is soft-spoken but his actions speak loudly. He laughs easily, hugs naturally, and has more friends than one can count. Carol is an English teacher at the local community college. She speaks at least four languages and has a nurturing touch, worthy of a professional counselor. Her ripped jeans, earthy demeanor, and love for all things recycled makes her part of a humble minority in a city where too many people are living life as if it were a runway show. Her wit is refreshingly sharp, her intellect acutely refined, her language skills impressive, and her love for justice inspiring. Just like Noel, she laughs easily, hugs naturally, and makes long-lasting friendships.

I first met Noel back in 1992, after Hurricane Andrew blew through South Florida and devastated thousands of homes. He was readily equipped with a willingness for service. Since then, Noel has made weekly, if not daily, appearances in the same service-oriented posture. He is the ultimate example of living a life devoted to justice. Noel and Carol are extremely modest people. I knew that, unlike other successful people who speak freely about their accomplishments, I would have to pull the words from them.

The morning of the interview we met at Noel's home, a small, eco-friendly, wood-frame house. It was a chilly morning by Miami standards—fifty-five degrees—when almost any south Floridian would be dressed in warm clothes. Nonetheless, we all wanted to enjoy the weather, for we knew all too well that it would not last. We sat outside, in his xeriscaped yard (xeriscaping is landscaping that reduces the need for supplemental water from irrigation) and began the conversation while their dog, Riley, petitioned for our love with his big, begging eyes.

Guillermo: Carol, what faith did you grow up in, and how would you describe your faith today?

Carol: I grew up Episcopalian. I feel connected to Christianity because that is what I know best. I also embrace Buddhist principles of compassion and service. I also was influenced by my father and his commitment to social justice issues [*laughs*].

Guillermo: Noel, is it fair to say you grew up in the United Church of Christ?

Noel: Well, yes, since junior high when my parents left the Presbyterian church and took us to Coral Gables Congregational Church (CGCC). My grandfather was a Presbyterian minister, but something must have happened for my family to switch allegiance. However, I was but a sprouting teenager and not part of those decisions.

Guillermo: How does your faith inspire your activism?

Noel: The community we have at CGCC is very active, and seeing everything that people are doing to make this world a better place inspires me to become active. If you take a look at Miami-Dade County as a whole, the number of problems we have, and look for the number of people who are doing something, it's actually not much. At least from what I can see. So the church is fertile ground to get people together to create some change.

Guillermo: So are you saying the faith community of the church is what gives you the motivation to be an activist?

Noel: Well, just the education alone has been very formative. Ideas get developed, discussed, and before you know it we're doing something. Also, the church creates opportunities for action and change.

Carol: I feel that faith manifests itself in activism. You can't have faith without putting it into action somehow. I don't call myself an activist; I can't claim that title. I'm more of a "wanna-be" activist. I want to be involved in making right the social inequities that surround us . . . . I wake up in the morning feeling blessed and the first question of the day is, "What can I do today to make someone's life better?" And the church provides for me the opportunity to answer that question.

Guillermo: Cool. Well, the two of you have a lifestyle that is not common. (*They nod.*) You both have a worldview that is not common. Can we start naming it? You're both vegans, right?

Carol: I've slipped here and there with a little dairy and little seafood . . . but I have recommitted myself to being a vegan.

Guillermo: For how many years have you guys been at this?

Carol: I have not eaten chicken, beef, or pork for thirteen years. I want my choices to be kinder and gentler to all life forms and think of their needs above mine.

Noel: We're eating lower on the food chain.

Guillermo: What about you, Noel?

Noel: Twenty-one years.

Guillermo: To point the obvious, veganism or vegetarianism is not a Christian doctrine. So what is it about your faith that pushes you toward being a vegan?

Noel: That's a good point. I can't really say Jesus was a vegetarian, but he tried to live a simple lifestyle and stand up for his beliefs. His compassion and love for others makes a great role model for vegans.

Guillermo: Has your faith broken away from the biblical stories in order to help you become a vegan?

Noel: Well, the Bible is full of violence, but it also has a lot of hope and love. In many sections it's a war story. I don't think our faith is based on violence, and our faith no longer includes animal sacrifices. So I would say the biblical stories represent the evolution of becoming more noble creatures, and the story is not finished.

Humans have the capacity to eat whatever they want, and for the most part we do. It is highly unlikely that a person would starve to death with a bunch of chickens running around. But that's not the world we live in now. That's not our reality. Chicken now comes to us as one of the many choices in the refrigerated aisles of the grocery stores.

Guillermo: But tell me about your personal understanding of God and how that personal understanding has moved you to be a vegetarian.

Noel: My personal understanding is that of a loving God. And there's nothing loving about how food is prepared for us in the twenty-first century. I say that because we know how food preparation contributes to animal cruelty.

Carol: I feel the same way. I think many of the choices we make as a society are violent and non-loving. I don't believe Jesus would condone a meat-eating lifestyle, at least in the way that meat is prepared today. I want to be a truly compassionate person, and that includes animals, fish of the sea, as well as my neighbors here on Earth.

Guillermo: Well, there's something to be said about the context of Jesus. I don't know if the animals were treated with respect, but I do know shepherds slept with their flock. Often the animals lived inside the same dwelling of the humans. That proximity will change how a person understands an animal.

Carol: For most people there's a huge disconnect. They don't know how a cow ends up in their fridge as steak. We never say we're eating cow. So at the subconscious level we give ourselves permission to eat meat because we don't name it as an animal. When I want to eat broccoli, I name it that way. For cow, it ends up being rib-eye, or cheeseburger . . . not to mention everything that happens to the cow and to the environment in order for that rib-eye to be served on a plate: the amount of water that is used and polluted, the pesticide that is spread on the field . . .

Guillermo: Let's transition into that. Carol, are you an environmentalist?

Carol: Well, in many ways I am, but I don't really live it and breathe it the way a true environmentalist would. I don't ride my bike to work the way Noel does. I turn on the air conditioner during the warmer months. But I'm trying to be more intentional about my actions and my carbon footprint.

Noel [*with a playful smile*]: She also uses clothes to the bitter end (*pointing at her ripped jeans*), until they are full of holes and beyond recycling.

Carol [*laughing*]: Well, I like my jeans. Besides, you guys get to see my skin.

Guillermo: Is this a fashion statement?

Carol: I dressed like this for you [*laughter*]. But clothing is also part of the issue. How clothes are made is also an environmental issue.

Noel: I think that "environmentalist" is possibly one of the hardest labels to wear. Only because of the hypocrisy of being here . . . being here is taking a toll on the planet. When the human population was five hundred million, the planet could absorb human behavior without a problem. When the human population is seven billion, we are causing some serious wear and tear to this planet.

        Environmentalism is a goal. It's one of those unachievable goals. Compare it to being a Christian. It's like if someone would say the only true Christians are those who don't sin. Well, we all are aspiring to be better. Environmentalists have the same goal. We aspire to live in better harmony with our environment, but we know we are far from perfect.

Guillermo: Have you found that the way you live your life inspires others to look at their own lifestyle and make changes?

Carol: It certainly generates a lot of discussion. For one reason or another people get curious. It's inevitable. People want to know why I don't eat this or don't do that, and sometimes they feel they have to defend their habits and choices even though I haven't said one word about them.

        I remember one day I was reading this book, *What's in Your Milk?* and I brought it to my class. I spoke with my students about how milk gets into the cartons, and how it's a violent process for the cows. I had some students on that day swear they wouldn't touch dairy again.

It's an educational process. If people can begin to question and talk about these things that we take for granted, lives change. You know, we move through the day not questioning what we are doing. We just accept that for breakfast it's good to have a glass of milk and for dinner a steak. Well, is it really? And when people ask me about my choices, it gets them to think about theirs. So, yeah.

Noel: Carol mentioned that we have to be intentional. I want to say that too many of us are living the lives of a lemming. We just run with the rest of the crowd, not sure why we are running, but we do it because everyone else is doing it too. That is until we see that we're going over a cliff. So here we are with the rest of the world on a path that is leading us the wrong way. Do we have the ability to stop? I think we do. We have to be intentional about all we do, and not be a lemming. We have to think about what we eat, what we drive, what we wear. I have to tell you that when gas prices go up, I get more questions about my bicycle and riding it to work: "So, what route do you take?"

It's definitely on the radar screen. Carol and I are always fielding questions about our dietary choices: "Where do you get your protein?" The conversation is there. Some people may not be able to make changes to their lifestyle, but the fact they are asking questions is important. It's the first step.

Guillermo: Well, I think you're being modest. I think your lifestyle is making a bigger impact than you give yourself credit for.

Carol: Yeah, I think so too. One thing about Noel, he's so loving in the way that he expresses his activism. You know, it's easy to get mad. We can look at people who are eating beef and berate them. "Don't you know what you're doing is bad for the earth?" Noel is all about the direction, not the perfection. He tells people it's about taking small steps in the right direction, and this makes people consider what they are doing. There's so much compassion in his approach that I find it beautiful.

Guillermo: There's also something to be said about willpower. Like, I already know everything I need to know, but how do I build my internal willpower to follow through with the decision to not eat beef? And often, I'm good for two or three months, and then I'll falter. A craving will come over me . . . overwhelming.

Noel: Would that be the same craving that can be compared to someone who craves an alcoholic drink, or a cigarette or a drug?

Guillermo: I've read that there's an addiction to meat and meat-related substances. So if that is true, the challenge is more than about providing information. It now moves into the arena of providing resources to overcome a meat addiction.

Noel: The other thing is that we're talking about this from the environmental perspective. Most people who go into veganism do it for a compassionate reason, for a love of the animals. Then there are the health reasons to consider.

Carol: Isn't there a study that states people who stay with a vegetarian diet are those who approach it from the point of compassion for the animals?

Noel: Yes, I read that. And people who go into it for health reasons may slip and return to a meat-eating diet, especially when they lost the weight or their cholesterol levels dropped. They think, *Okay, now I'm better. I can return to eating steak and it'll be all right.*

Guillermo: There's a new wave of activism sweeping through the younger generation. As a person who lives a justice-centered life, what advice would you give a person who is thinking about activism?

Noel [*smiling*]: Question authority. The next generation is always good about questioning the authority of their parents, but often it stops there. Consider how easily we can be manipulated by those who are in power. So it's important to always question. Then it gets back to being intentional.

Carol: Yeah.

Noel: If you are being intentional about something, then great for you. But if you are just doing it because everyone else is doing it, or because that is how you were taught, then you are forfeiting your power of choice.

Carol: I agree about the whole thing of being intentional, but how do you teach kids who have ADD and all these video games and distractions about being intentional? How do you tell the whole society to slow down and be intentional?

Guillermo: Anything else you want to offer about lifestyle and justice?

Noel: Well, a friend of mine—some time ago called me a hypocrite. I was saying certain things and doing another. And I found that it really struck a nerve with me. I found the need to be more intentional as a way of avoiding the hypocrisy in my own life. (*Looking up.*) There's a beautiful cardinal behind you.

Carol: Oh, yeah. Male. Look at his colors!

Guillermo: We don't get too many cardinals in South Florida.

Noel: We get a few, but not like we used to. I have a bird feeder up front. That helps to bring them. So, I was talking about . . .

Guillermo: The hypocrisy in your life . . .

Noel: Yeah. That was an early motivator for me. It made me think about what I was doing. I was influenced by people along the way like my father. He was always questioning authority and examining the way we live. He was a real role model for me. (*Looking at Carol.*) Like your father was for you.

Carol: Absolutely.

Guillermo: Yeah. You both had fathers who were justice-centered activists, and also men of faith.

Noel: Very much so.

Carol: That's why we take our grandkids to Occupy Miami [*laughs*]. It's something you have to pass down. It's an important value. Noel and I had this conversation last night. I asked him to help me figure out how I could volunteer my time this summer. I have this burning desire to make a difference. I have to go down to Haiti or something. It's part of my DNA now, and how do we create a society like that? It's hard to introduce it to people who don't know what that means.

Noel: Speaking of the Occupy movement. I'm so impressed with the young people who attend these rallies. They are so well-versed with the issues and they can dialogue about them in ways that motivate change. It's inspiring to see young people with that focus. Unfortunately, I really feel that my generation dropped the ball. They had an opportunity during the 1960s and '70s to make a significant difference. Their eyes were open with the social revolution concepts, but in a matter of a few years they changed course. They started to make money or do whatever it was that became the distraction, and things are no better off now than when they started. In many ways they are worse.

Carol: There is a lot more to do. I look at Noel and then I look at myself and I think, *Oh my God, I have so much further to go.* But as we said earlier, it's not about the perfection, it's about the direction.

We reached a moment of uncomfortable silence and realized the day was getting colder. We laughed at ourselves. As true south Floridians we found ourselves cold in weather that the rest of the nation desired. Carol reached over to Noel for warmth and smiled. She needed his touch. Her love for him spilled over in that smile and he caught every drop of it. He looked at her and smiled back. For a second I sensed in their smiles an exchange of loving desires.

That was my cue to depart. As I left, I found myself thinking about them, their commitment to veganism, and their efforts to reduce their carbon footprint and to enjoy each other's love. If only we could inspire more people to live and love like they do, the world would be a better place.

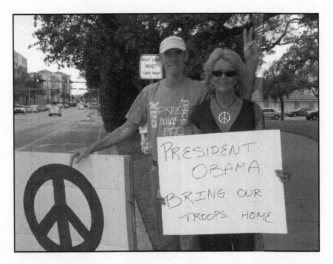

Carol and Noel at a Peace Rally (April, 2009)

CHAPTER 5

Generosity, the Inspiring Force in Activism

The person who does not practice generosity is like a blacksmith's bellows: breathing but not living.

~Irish proverb

The word generosity did not enter the vocabulary of the western world until the late-sixteenth century. It comes from the French *generoux,* which in turn comes from the Latin *genus,* meaning "class" or "kind of thing." Generosity initially meant the act of giving by those who were born into higher economic classes or aristocratic circles. The generous were those who had resources and could afford to give. Accurate translations of the Bible do not show the use of the word "generous." In the first century, the closest Hebrew words to it were *tzedakah*, meaning "charity," and *chanan,*[19] meaning "merciful" or "graceful." Biblical language may not use the word generous, but there are multiple passages that indicate the biblical authors had a deep understanding of it. The Gospel story of the Good Samaritan describes in detail the embodiment of generosity.

In John's first letter (1 John 3:16) in the Christian Bible, there is a passage that describes generosity: *By this we know love—that he laid down his life for us, and we ought to lay down our lives for our brothers. But if anyone has the world's goods and sees his brother in need, yet closes his heart against him, how does God's love abide in him?*

This passage, as well as others, describes generosity through the act of love. Love is linked to generosity because those who love are supposed to be generous. Healthy expressions of love are generous. However, we must be very careful how we use the word, *love*, because "love" is too often misunderstood, misused, and manipulated for wrongful ends. Too many people have deep emotional scars created by those who "loved" them. I have witnessed too many "loving" homes produce unhealthy expressions of love that smother and control. How many parents have ruined the lives of their children with unhealthy expressions of love? How many people have manipulated and dominated using love as justification?

Another concern with the use of the word love is that it cannot be measured effectively. What is love for one person might be abusive sex for another. Consequently, I prefer to move the focus from love to faith.

Faith is a needed component in spiritual activism. We must have faith that the time and energy we are putting into an effort of justice will have a positive impact. People with faith give generously because they recognize they too have been recipients of generosity. Most importantly, faith reassures us that we can give without fear of losing. People who are afraid will not give. They will hold on to possessions for fear of losing them. Generosity is an act of faith. It is easily observed, recognized, and measured. It is a behavior that has positive impact. Only a person with a generous spirit can give without expecting something in return. Generosity allows for the spirit of forgiveness, which in turn keeps us from falling into the trap of anger and resentment. When generosity is practiced, it brings out in others hope and joy. It feels good to be generous because we know we have been part of something good and the recipient of our gift is better for it.

Putting the word love aside, it could be argued that the basic teachings of every religion can be reduced to generosity. Compassion, a virtue taught in all major religions, also flows from the generous heart. The compassionate person places her priorities before the needs of the other. To have compassion is to remove your own ego and risk a loss for the sake of another. Consequently, the Spiritual Activist is compassionate when he is generous with money, time, praise, and kindness. The opposite of generosity is selfishness. The opposite of faith is fear. Faith is to generosity what fear is to selfishness.

Listen to the words of a Wrongful Activist and we can hear self-serving and self-centered reasoning. If faith and generosity are the identifying marks of a Spiritual Activist, then fear and selfishness are the marks of a Wrongful Activist. Selfishness, as a behavior, is easily recognized and contrasts sharply with generosity. It may lead to a wrongful behavior but not necessarily to an injustice.

Selfishness is not the same as greed. Many selfish people can be generous, for deep down inside they are good. It is fear that is keeping them from giving. Greed, however, is an intentional and malicious state of being that will lead to a deliberate injustice.

Selfish behavior is often demonized, but as Spiritual Activists we must develop a deeper understanding of irrational fear and how it leads people to be less than generous. When we fear we build walls to protect ourselves from the perceived enemy. When we fear, we seek to protect our children from that which we don't understand. A Spiritual Activist seeks to help people identify their fears, overcome them and begin to act faithfully. This can only happen if we believe people to be inherently good. To be generous is to view people as being good, even if they are speaking wrongful words that stem from their fearful condition. We live in an era of polarizing diatribes that promote fear and demonize the other. It is time to embrace a spirit of generosity and stop the demonization, or else further problems will ensue. When we make the effort to understand the emotions, the fear, the root motivations behind people then we can be agents of change. Generosity is the element Spiritual Activists must swim in.

Northern Ireland: A History Lesson We Should Heed

Consider the historic fight between the Catholics and the Protestants in Northern Ireland that lasted well more than two hundred years. To non-Christians, this battle seemed irrational, since Catholics and Protestants have more in common than not. The true issues were poverty and oppression from years of British rule, but it was the religious differences between them that provided the scapegoat for justifying the violence. There were serious humanitarian concerns, but the only thing they saw was the demon Catholic or the demon Protestant. There were serious words to be spoken, but the only thing anyone could hear were the religious insults tossed like hand grenades.

The housing and humanitarian crisis in Belfast and other cities led to many justified protests, but the hatred toward their religious differences kept the leaders from reasonable dialogue. Although several agreements were reached and peace always seemed to be at hand, it was not until February 5, 2010, with the signing of the Hillsborough Castle Agreement,[20] that a peaceful accord was reached. Curiosity begs the question: What kept these two nations, these two neighboring communities, from coexisting in peace? From an outsider's point of view, they had more reasons to work out their differences than to keep fighting. Yet they kept the fight for more than two hundred years, and tens of thousands of people died in the process; not to mention the millions of people who suffered the ills and pains of poverty and war. So what was the impasse that kept them from working out their differences in a peaceful manner? It was the wrongful demonization of that which made them different. The Catholics demonized the Protestants and vice versa. Neither would approach a dialogue with a spirit of generosity and forgiveness. The lesson to be learned here is that when we demonize our opponents and those who are different, we stop listening.

It is sad to say, and even sadder to realize, that a similar polarization has been taking root in America. America will most likely not go the path of Northern Ireland for a variety of factors, but we are in danger of suffering a similar fate due to the growing demonization, the irrational fear and the ripple effects of negativity. Wrongful Activists on both sides of the political aisle are demonizing each other, preventing fruitful dialogue, and promoting a culture of disrespect, dishonor, and violence. The hostility is palpable in the rhetoric used by politicians and political commentators. Listen to left-leaning commentators criticize the Republicans. Switch the channel and listen to the right-leaning commentators lambaste the Democrats. Both sides are entrenched in their point of view, accusing the other of sabotage and other malicious deeds. Anger begets anger. Suspiciousness begets more suspiciousness. The ripple effect is that these negative attributes have been assimilated by the people. Communities of Republicans and communities of Democrats cannot work together, let alone converse.

In the span of thirty-three months—January 2009 to October 2011—two activist movements swept through the United States, pulling people into polar extremes of the same issue. One movement was led by a coalition of conservative thinkers; the other by liberal and progressive activists. I am referring to the Tea Party and the Occupy Wall Street movements. Both were addressing frustrations with the US government but from opposite views, which led to opposing coalitions. Even though the participants of both movements were suffering from the same economic illness, they were not able to build common ground because they held on to their differences too tightly. Each movement demonized the other, and the harmful rhetoric widened the growing gap. It was difficult to not take a side, but to do so was to fall into the trap that leads to demonization. Both movements had good people involved with legitimate concerns and with good intentions. Yet both movements were appealing to different demographic groups in the nation.

"Take Back America" versus "We Are the 99%": The Pendulum Swings

We cannot speak about activism in the twenty-first century without analyzing two grassroots movements: We Are the 99% and the Take Back America campaign. The latter emerged from the Tea Party protest movement, the former from Occupy Wall Street. Both movements had strong reactions against the government bailout of banks and financial institutions that occurred in 2008 and 2009. Both movements were inherently nonviolent, lacked clear leadership in the early stages, had a grassroots component, and had economic and political implications. Regardless of these similarities, there were some marked differences between them. As we look at the timeline of these movements, we can also see how the Occupy Wall Street movement emerged, almost unintentionally, as a reaction to the Tea Party.

The Tea Party movement began within weeks of President Obama's inauguration, with protesters carrying signs that read "Take Back America." Consequently, it quickly spawned the Take Back America campaign. If we were to assess the movement only on this slogan, we could read the fear that is behind it. "Take back America" strongly implies a fear of the future and a longing for an era that felt good. Most observers were not sure what this group wanted to take America back to, but it is obvious that it reflects a fear of what lies ahead. As discussed earlier, fear leads to protectionism, which in turn may lead to wrongful behavior. Critics of the Tea Party saw the Take Back America slogan as racist and causing great divisions in the social fabric of the country. Although bigotry cannot be excluded from this argument, the underlying issue at work is fear of the many changes a black president with a Muslim middle name would create. Proof of this argument is the timing of the campaign's birth. It emerged on the American landscape when the Republican Party was defeated by a landslide when Barack Hussein Obama became the nation's president in the 2008 elections. Further proof was the skyrocketing sales of rifles, guns, and other firearms by people who identify with the Tea Party. What would lead whole groups of church-going, middleclass, hardworking Americans to purchase five and six guns at one time? The answer is obvious: fear.

In all fairness, the Tea Party movement as a whole cannot be blamed for the few extremists who attended these events and held up signs with racist and hateful messages. There were good people attending the Tea Party rallies. Yet, at many rallies hateful epithets and messages were part of the scenery. This begs the question: What underlying conditions were present that would allow for this behavior to emerge?

From 2009 through most of 2010, it was a difficult time for most Americans to remain neutral. The debates and heated arguments would push people to take a side. When Tea Party members were accused of racism they would counter by saying that the rise of the movement was due to the unprecedented debt the nation was incurring and the government bailout of the financial institutions. Critics of the Tea Party would then ask, "Where was your anger when the Bush administration quadrupled the deficit and threw us into two wars?" This question was always trumped by the historic tragedy of 9/11. To argue against the War on Terror was seen not only as unpatriotic but also as un-American. Needless to say, the Tea Party movement grew because its message was reaching many homes. Many of these homes had other concerns that in some form overlapped with the Take Back America campaign.

In the latter part of 2009, other social conservative values quickly became part of the Tea Party identity. Nursed by Wrongful Activists, Tea Party followers and the Take Back America campaign set their sights on the immigrants, the GLBT community, and the Islamic people, who wanted to peacefully exercise their constitutional right of the first amendment. A spirit of selfishness spread throughout the land, intended to prevent those who were perceived as "different" from enjoying the same human rights enjoyed by the majority. At Tea Party rallies throughout the nation, Wrongful Activists delivered speeches that were laced with fear against these "enemies" of America who were threatening our children. Wrongful Activists embraced images of grizzly bears defending their cubs—possibly one of the most violent images in nature. Such language can only promote violence and stir the masses to rise against their peaceful neighbors, be they immigrant, Muslim, or gay. Consequently, xenophobia, homophobia, and Islamophobia became hallmarks of this movement.[21]

The rise of the Wrongful Activist coincided with the Take Back America campaign, when other people started to repeat the same negative and violent message that marked its identity. In July 2010, the Rev. Terry Jones, a self-trained minister of the Christian faith[22], became a Wrongful Activist when he announced he would burn multiple copies of the Quran before television cameras. When confronted, Jones defended his logic and did not apologize. To the rest of America, the moral dissonance was deafening. In March 2011 Jones carried out his threat, sparking a violent protest in Afghanistan that resulted in the death of seven UN officials.[23] Is there a citizen in our fair nation who would not hold Jones accountable for these deaths?

The year 2010 was a stressful one. It began with the landmark decision of the Supreme Court in Citizens United vs. Federal Elections Commission, to undo the McCain-Feingold Act and declare corporations to be people. There was no doubt that special interest groups were going to openly fund political campaigns. While progressives protested the judicial decision, Tea Party protests across the country moved the rhetoric to a new extreme, characterizing President Obama as the anti-Christ or a modern-day Hitler. These repeated accusations had many people concerned—and as we know all too well, violent language creates the framework for violent action. Sadly, too many people remained silent, not knowing that their silence was interpreted as an endorsement. Silence grew into apathy, and many did not turn out to vote in the 2010 elections. The consequence of such apathy allowed Tea Party supporters to win several key political races and thus become a powerful political influence. While many citizens were suffering from apathy, newly elected legislators were like prize fighters entering the ring, ready to fight for their political goals and beliefs. This aggressive spirit escalated, eventually leading to an impasse in the legislative process.

In 2011, teachers and other civil servants were blamed for the budget deficits around the nation, while corporations like GE, Wells Fargo, and Carnival Cruise Lines continued to receive tax-free benefits. This blatant favoritism of wealthy corporations was justified by arguments that did not hold up to public scrutiny. As the heated dispute reached screaming levels in the halls of Congress, it became obvious to the listening public that the well-being of the nation had fallen in priority to an irrational desire to antagonize the president. No other moment exemplified this selfish behavior better than that during the summer of 2011 when President Obama called for the raise of the debt ceiling and conservative legislators blocked every proposal. Many US citizens were deeply disappointment with this wrongful spirit that eventually led to the downgrading of the nation's credit rating in August 2011.

It was here that the Occupy Wall Street (OWS) movement was born. It emerged from the frustrating realization that the political process was going to continue on a downward spiral of deterioration until the working class would be held in perpetual servitude to a ruling upper class receiving TARP bonuses, tax credits, and favorable economic policies. The different groups that did the initial organizing for OWS got their inspiration from various sources: previous "Occupy" protests that began in 2007 and were still being led by Voices for Creative Nonviolence; the occupy movement in Spain, Toma la Plaza, which occurred about twelve weeks earlier led by *Los Indignados* ("The Outraged");[24] a

Spanish manual on activism: *How to Cook a Nonviolent Revolution*; the Arab Spring; and, of course, *Adbusters'* call to flood Wall Street with twenty thousand people, but ninety-thousand showed up.[25] Conservative critics of OWS stated that the occupiers were just a bunch of angry college kids with no understanding of the economic issues. There was a general annoyance that the occupiers were not unified in their message. It was not clear what they stood for or wanted. The variety of signs calling for a variety of policy changes, ranging from the Free Gaza movement to additional taxation of the upper 1 percent, kept critics stating that the OWS movement was decentralized, unfocused, and run by anarchists. Conservative critics were also quick to point out the pot-smoking, tattooed, and Communist feel of every drum circle at OWS.

People who were willing to investigate further saw something else. Yes, it was a movement against modern finance and "corporatocracy."[26] Yes, they were tired of politicians pandering to the wealthy. But behind these words the root of a deeper issue was surfacing. The OWS protests reflected a deep dissatisfaction with the general direction of society. OWS was calling out for society to refuse the shallow commercialism, monetary idolatry, and institutionalization of inequality that began in the third quarter of the twentieth century and had reached intolerable and unsustainable levels. OWS was calling for a boycott of modern American society. This boycott brought together two unlikely populations: the new generation of educated, debt-ridden, not-wanting-to-inherit-their parents'-mess protesters, and the homeless community.

The spirit of generosity at OWS welcomed the homeless into their camps. After decades of being pushed out, homeless people were now part of a community; part of the 99 percent. Homeless men and women were now acknowledged and not disregarded as worthless beggars. It was the perfect humanitarian statement. Despite the many decades of dealing with homelessness, many Americans treat the homeless like unwanted, diseased beggars. This prejudicial view of the homeless was evident in the critics of OWS, who openly stated the protesters were nothing more than organized, smelly beggars. Yet other people saw protesters who were very clear on what they wanted: first, to be heard. ("We Are the 99%" was a loud cry for recognition.) Secondly, they demanded government be generous with its form of governance.

Ten weeks into the movement, an OWS vision statement was created:

> We envision: [1] a truly free, democratic, and just society; [2] where we, the people, come together and solve our problems by consensus; [3] where people are encouraged to take personal and collective responsibility and participate in decision-making; [4] where we learn to live in harmony and embrace principles of toleration and respect for diversity and the differing views of others; [5] where we secure the civil and human rights of all from violation by tyrannical forces and unjust governments; [6] where political and economic institutions work to benefit all, not just

the privileged few; [7] where we provide full and free education to everyone, not merely to get jobs but to grow and flourish as human beings; [8] where we value human needs over monetary gain, to ensure decent standards of living without which effective democracy is impossible; [9] where we work together to protect the global environment to ensure that future generations will have safe and clean air, water and food supplies, and will be able to enjoy the bounty of nature that past generations have enjoyed.[27]

In reading this vision statement, the practical observer may ask, "But how will this help with the mortgage crisis? How can this idealistic vision reform government so I won't have to foreclose on my home and my life?" The effect OWS had on government may not be measurable for several years, but it managed to change the national conversation. Before OWS, only well-read people in the field of economics knew the wealth distribution in the nation. Within thirty days of the start of the movement, it was the subject of every major news network.

In reading the vision statement of OWS, one can see the focus on improving society and the world. Critics of this statement claim that it is flowery socialism. In contrast, the Tea Party movement had listed its own "core principles" outlining the reduction of government, taxes, and business regulation as essential in order to be an American Patriot.

The Tea Party list their core principles:[28]

FISCAL RESPONSIBILITY means not overspending, and not burdening our children and grandchildren with our bills . . . A more fiscally responsible government will take fewer taxes from our paychecks.

CONSTITUTIONALLY LIMITED GOVERNMENT means power resides with the people and not with the government. Governing should be done at the most local level possible where it can be held accountable. America's founders believed: that government power should be limited, enumerated, and constrained by our Constitution. Tea Party Patriots agree. The American people make this country great, not our government.

FREE MARKET ECONOMICS made America an economic superpower that for at least two centuries provided subsequent generations of Americans more opportunities and higher standards of living . . . . Failures in government programs and government-controlled financial markets helped spark the worst financial crisis since the Great Depression. Further government interventions and takeovers have made this Great

Recession longer and deeper. A renewed focus on free markets will lead to a more vibrant economy creating jobs and higher standards of living for future generations.

Issue	Tea Party	Occupy
Government	Needs to be reduced.	Needs to be expanded.
Military	Needs to be expanded. Portrayed as promoters of democracy and American values.	Needs to be reduced. Portrayed as protecting interests of US corporations abroad.
Taxation	Decrease taxes, especially of the top quintile.	Increase taxes, especially of the top quintile.
Capitalism	A virtue that should not be regulated. It is un-American to speak against it.	It needs regulation. It has run amok and it's America's duty to regulate it.
The Wealthy	Have benefited from their own hard work and should be given taxation benefits because they create jobs.	Have benefited from a systemic injustice that gives access, resources and unfair advantages to the wealthy.
The Poor	People who need to work harder and study better. It is their own fault they are poor.	People who have fallen into a perpetual state of poverty due to the policies created by the wealthy.

Immigration	Close the border and deport all illegal immigrants. Immigrants portrayed as stealing American jobs and resources.	Amnesty for immigrants and reform the immigration laws to benefit everyone. Immigrants portrayed as an asset to America.
Islamic People	Portrayed as enemies of the nation who should not build their mosque in Manhattan.	Portrayed as our neighbors and friends who deserve to enjoy the 1st amendment.
Gay Rights	Portray GLBT people as sick who have chosen a lifestyle that erodes the basic family values of America.	Portray GLBT people as human beings who seek the rights heterosexual people take for granted.
Banking and Finance Sector	Too big to fail, so it needs to be protected.	Too big to fail, so it needs to be broken into smaller banks.
Labor Unions	Portrayed as the problem that keeps corporations from increasing profits.	Portrayed as the solution to keep corporations from exploiting the workers.

The OWS movement is unfolding as I write. It is not certain what the next phase of the OWS movement will look like. Many hope a new generation of leaders and activists will emerge. As predicted by anyone who has been part of any movement, the future of OWS rests on its ability to become organized. Some fear that if it becomes organized it will be the beginning of its end.

Nonetheless, several branches of the OWS have begun to form a political organization with OWS values. It will be important for Spiritual Activists to be watchful of this transition.

Greed has a way of showing its ugly head everywhere. Although I admire the Occupy Wall Street movement, I am painfully aware that it too is subject to the infiltration of Wrongful Activists. As mentioned earlier, people are often easily manipulated by wrongful words that promote wrongful actions. As the pendulum swings, we have seen the rise of the Wrongful Activist—but it is time for its fall. This is a new era, with new opportunities. It is time for the rise of the Spiritual Activist.

Interview: Faith, Generosity, and Vision

As long as society is anti-gay, then it will seem like being gay is antisocial.

~Joseph Francis

In 1993, an organization named SAVE Dade was formed for the purposes of ending legalized discrimination against the GLBT community in Miami, Florida. For five years the organization worked to have a human rights ordinance passed that would include sexual orientation as one of the categories that cannot be discriminated against. A leader emerged: Jorge Mursuli, who became the face and voice of SAVE Dade.

I first met Jorge in 1997 when he was in need of Hispanic clergy to endorse the ordinance. Because of the overwhelming Hispanic presence in South Florida, my progressive theological contribution in Spanish was required. The ordinance passed in 1998 and SAVE Dade survived several attempted repeals of the ordinance. It was an important step forward for the gay rights movement, and I'm glad Jorge asked me to be part of it. The experience connected us, transcending any differences and creating common ground. Regardless of how much time may pass, we still greet each other like the old friends we are.

Most people take an immediate liking to Jorge. His smile radiates a genuine hospitality that is disarming. The lasting impression of Jorge is that he is articulate, intelligent, funny, and kind. His passion for justice easily emerges in conversation while inviting laughter, deep thought, and the best one has to offer.

I met Jorge for the interview at a low-budget Cuban restaurant. After ordering our food I asked, "What role did your faith play in the justice effort of seeking human rights for the GLBT community?"

Jorge: You know, I am not sure I've ever considered what we did over at SAVE from a faith perspective. Well, you know I grew up Catholic like most Cubans. I did the whole Catholic thing, you know. But I had a falling out with the church when I became aware of my sexuality. I remember telling the priest that I thought I was gay, and I wanted to get some words of guidance from him. I needed something beyond the liturgical words that we repeat Sunday after Sunday. So I was extremely disappointed.

Guillermo What did the priest say?

Jorge: I don't remember the words exactly. It was more than thirty years ago. He was all about the rehab, as if I could be conditioned to feel otherwise.

            But let me fast forward to the time of SAVE. I remember when the ordinance was going to be filed . . . being up late at night, unable to sleep, and thinking about the opposition we were going to face. I was up at night thinking about all the hatred that was coming our way . . . and I was scared . . . to my core. It was the first time in my life when I placed it all in God's hands. You asked me, "How did my faith play a role?" Well, I think I found my faith at that time, 'cause I just put it all in God's hands.

The waiter arrived with a tray of food. Jorge and I looked at the bowls of black beans and our mouths watered. As the waiter placed our food on the table, Jorge spoke, almost apologetically, about the baby steps of SAVE Dade.

Jorge: In the beginning, people just thought we were poorly organized queers. And to a certain degree they were right. We had no clue what was coming our way. As time went on we became more politically savvy. In the beginning we were doing things because we knew it was the right thing to do, but we had no idea how the political system worked.

As for my faith, I was doing this because I wanted a whole life . . . and that includes job, faith, family— everything. I didn't want a pseudo life, which is what many gay people did back then. It was the '90s, and back then gay men went around pretending. My parents came to this country in search of freedom. They lost too much in Cuba and they worked their asses off in this country so I could have more. I wasn't about to piss it all away for a pseudo life. I wanted a whole life. I wanted . . . the truth.

I was once talking with Bishop—you know, the guy from Overtown? . . . He was questioning the whole movement. I said, "Bishop, for those of us who want to follow Jesus Christ, where do we go? Tell us what do we do and where do we go? Short of celibacy,

I can't choose who I love. I can choose sex or not having sex, but I can't choose who I love. What are you asking us to do?" You can't just cherry-pick 90 percent of your flock and let the others fall by the wayside.

That got him. That really got him. Instead of debating the Bible with the bishop, I approached it from the point of love.

Guillermo: You got him to realize that the gay community feels just as deeply as the straight community.

Jorge: Exactly. We both knew people are innately good. My faith helped me develop that point of view. It also allowed me to be curious. If there is someone who is in opposition of LGBT equality, but I think he is good at heart, I am curious as to what it is he is afraid of.

When I was advocating in the middle of this effort I would initially assume people were innately good. If you believe people are good, you can approach them.

I had a conversation with Alejandro Aguirre from *El Diario las Americas.* He only wanted to give me twenty minutes and we ended up talking for more than three hours. He said to me, "Jorge, I like to walk down Lincoln Road with my family. And when I see a store with chains and whips on the front window all I can think of is that I don't want my kids to see this. It's about my kids and protecting them. If I have to deny someone his or her rights to protect my kids, then that is what I will do."

I thought, *Okay . . . some honesty . . . now we're talking.*

So I said to him, "I agree with you. I don't want my niece and nephew seeing those stores either. But what this ordinance will do has nothing to do with people putting whips on their front window. I completely understand; you and I would do the same thing. I don't want some 'hoochie mama' making out with some dude in front of my niece and nephew. You would be a bad parent if you allowed your kids to be exposed to that kind of behavior. But this ordinance is not about the storefront windows on Lincoln Road. This ordinance is about people enjoying the same rights that are afforded in the constitution. It's not about the whips or chains or the people who practice bestiality. If the ordinance loses, it's not going to stop the hoochie mama from doing her thing on Lincoln Road." We got past the rhetoric, and through honesty we made a lot of progress that day. It was an important day for me.

Guillermo: How important was his support to the movement?

Jorge: Very important, because that newspaper is a very conservative paper. He sent reporters to cover the movement and to ask the questions with integrity . . . in a holistic way. He didn't promote the negative stereotypes of gay people. It was not a free ride by any stretch of the imagination, but at least we got the most-read newspaper in the Hispanic community to cover the story and to put in print what the issues were.

Guillermo: At one point you became the face and leader of SAVE Dade. When did that occur? Was it by chance?

Jorge: No. They elected me. Listen, I never started this thinking that I would end up doing it on a full-time basis. I entered the movement as a volunteer . . . one day I decided I needed to do something and volunteer . . . go lick envelopes somewhere. So I went to SAVE Dade as a volunteer and I worked hard, never thinking I would become a leader. But exposure to the activism, to knowing I could make a difference . . . it got me going. There was a moment when I realized that "this is what purpose is all about." That awareness is intoxicating—being purposeful is intoxicating.

Guillermo: Talk to me about the early stages. How did you guys strategize?

Jorge: In my backyard. There's a funny story about us trying to strategize while the mosquitoes were eating us alive.

Guillermo: How big a group was your strategizing team?

Jorge: About twenty. About ten people did the heavy lifting . . . . Back then the strategy was divided. I think my corporate training skills really helped me a lot. You know I was a corporate trainer? And I think that really helped me. Because we had the radical liberals who wanted to do a sit-in, and that works . . . it's a trick . . . a good trick that works. And then there were the behind-the-scenes people . . . keep it low . . . work with the politicians behind the scenes.

In the end we realized that this effort did not belong to the team of twenty. It belonged to the whole community. But my contribution was keeping that balancing act, and all the voices at the table. I also thought it was important that we belong to mainstream organizations like the chamber (of commerce). That was my baby. As a result, there were some people who thought I was a "straight person wanna-be." But my strength was getting people who were not gay to join us.

Guillermo: Do you mean SAVE became a member of the Chamber?

Jorge: Absolutely. And as a member, I was able to speak to the Chamber about how it was good business practice to have the ordinance. Because, in the end, Miami needs the business of the gay community.

Guillermo: So did the Chamber make a supporting statement for the ordinance?

Jorge: Not at the time of the ordinance, but they did once the repeal was set in motion. But before the ordinance we had . . . you know, that's not true. They did put out a statement of support. We got the Chamber, we got the Beacon Council, the Miami-Dade Chamber which is the African American chamber. Yes, we got them all, because, in the end we needed a faith message, a business message, and a fairness message.

The fairness message was that we wanted to be treated equally. You helped us formulate the faith message. The business message was that discrimination is bad business. To say that Miami discriminates . . . it's bad for tourism. That's a hard one to pass up. So we got them all.

Guillermo: How much resistance did you face?

Jorge: I don't think I could do today what I did back then. It's totally different now in the gay movement. Listen, if someone is speaking against the GLBT community today, after all we've been through, you know that person is probably a bigot. Back then it was different. People were less informed. The discrimination was more overt and we came up against some significant resistance . . . Some of these people . . . they were disgusting.

There was this one guy, Nathaniel . . . I'm forgetting his full name. You'll remember him. Anyway, he stood up at a council meeting and said he knew that gay and lesbian people like to pee all over each other. I think he said defecate, but not one county official stood up and said to him, "That's out of line." Not one. What are you supposed to think at that moment? Was no one going to correct that statement at a public meeting?

And what about Eladio Armesto (1998 director of Take Back Miami) who was arrested for hitting his pregnant wife with a clothes hanger? He hit his wife with a hanger! It's a matter of public record. I mean the guy was a low life. And he was passing moral judgment on me? He was going to decide if I am good person? What kind of society is this? I mean really. Really!

Guillermo: So, you decided back then to take the high road.

Jorge: Exactly; that is my point. Do you see how easy I can go there? I mean, it can happen in two seconds. We had to face people who were portraying cartoon stereotypes. When that kind of stuff happens it's very easy to say, "Go screw yourself."

Jorge continued to speak while we ate. But the food ran out long before the conversation. The waiter cleared the table and we ordered Cuban coffee and flan.

Jorge: We started working on this issue back in '93. We submitted the first try for the ordinance back in '96 and it failed. We went back and licked our wounds. We reassembled, and I said to them, "Guys, this is not about what is true. This is not about what is real. This is about politics." And then it became a different story. And that's when I took the helm.

Guillermo: Before that it was run by committee?

Jorge: Yeah, by committee and a great guy, Damian Pardo.

Guillermo: So you guys are approaching your twenty-five-year anniversary?

Jorge: Amazing, isn't it? I see today's movement . . . I see that . . . for today . . . and I know that is not what you're writing about.

Guillermo: It is. Please.

Jorge: Well, we started talking about faith, and I have to get back to it. Because faith is at the core of self-respect. And it is self-respect that allows you to be kind to other people. It's all connected. Without self-respect there's no reason to be kind to other people. And kindness is a thread of generosity and curiosity. It's all part of the same fabric.

And the best example of what is happening today is the story of (New York Gov. Andrew) Cuomo.

There was this whole brouhaha when the president was refusing to generate an execute order around "Don't Ask, Don't Tell," which was clearly in the realm of possibility. The president was claiming he didn't want to set a legal precedent.

So members of the gay community said, "Wait a minute. Is my life not worth a legal precedent? This is the guy who promised us all the things he promised and now he's backing down?" No. No more. And that's when Get Equal came in. They started out angry, by design. Get Equal went about getting the donors to approach Cuomo at New York's last gubernatorial race. Cuomo responded by openly supporting same-sex marriage. This was going on at the same time the president was in New York raising money for the DNC. Cuomo raised three times more money from New York's gay community than the president. And when Cuomo openly voiced his support, you saw what happened. The people went out to the streets to say thank you. There was no message calculation. It was just a plain and loud thank you. Why? Because we are free human beings. Now that was a statement the president could not ignore.

The gay movement today cannot approach the issue with the same flexibility we did in the '90s. In today's day and age, unless you've been hiding under a rock, opposition to GLBT equality is a choice to discriminate. And that puts you in a very different category: "I'm not curious about you anymore." So it's a very different time and a different tactic. It's a little bit of Occupy, right? I'm a fifty-one-year-old man. When am I going to enjoy my human rights? When I'm about to die? I don't think so. I want it now. So I have to stand up and make noise.

Listen, if out of Occupy there can emerge a leader who paints the enemy in a human way, that redirects the anger to a sense of faith and hope for the future while sticking to his guns about the demands, then true change will come to this nation. My hope and my prayer is that out of Occupy we will find new leaders for this country. That somebody comes out of Occupy with a new paradigm.

Guillermo: I want to ask you one more question. If you were to offer advice to modern-day activists, regardless of what they are fighting for . . . what did you learn in your years of activism that can be a lesson for today's activist?

Jorge: Ultimately, you need to know you get more than you lose. But you do lose. And you have to be okay with that. You have to be willing to be okay because you never know if you are going to win or not. You can't get into it for the potential of glory. I don't know what the statistics are, but I'll bet you anything there are more failure than there are successes.

There's an innate challenge with being a visionary. The reason visionaries are so lauded in history is because they're shat on all the way up the ladder. Because in order for your vision to make it to the next step, it's likely you will bump into the vision of twelve other people in that same arena. Visionaries are loved after the fact. They are not loved during.

Everything I did during that ordinance was guided by a vision of what is right. I didn't know what I was doing. I didn't have a mentor. Nobody said to me, "This is what's going to happen." It was uncharted territory—on the gay side, in my personal life. Did you know that during the campaign the Christian Coalition was watching and photographing my freaking house? But it didn't matter. I was in it because I knew what was right.

That's why faith is important and that is why self-respect is important—because it makes you generous. Generosity makes you . . .

Guillermo: What you're saying is that in order to overcome the storms that are in every justice effort, you need these attributes.

Jorge: Exactly! Look, some of this is innate. I'm very fortunate and grateful to God to have had these traits. So I'm grateful. I'm immensely grateful to my parents because they instilled in me a sense of self-respect. They taught me to love myself and others. And that means I have to behave a certain way with myself and toward other people. And the way you expect for others to treat you well is by treating them well. And that helped me in my worst-case scenarios. When anti-gay activists like Eladio would insult me publicly and say the most horrible things to me—oh my God, horrible things they would say!—but I had to let it go and focus on the bigger picture, or else I would have gone down to his level. I had to stay in control, and the only thing I could control was my choice on how to respond to all the hateful words thrown at me.

In this line of work you get thirty to forty pinches a day. When you have a sense of generosity, all the pinches don't hurt so much. And it allows you to face another day. It allows you stay in the driver's seat. You can't do this kind of work if you can't stay in the driver's seat. It's a sort of anti-victim program. Otherwise you remain a victim all the while.

Guillermo: You spoke about failure and the difficulties of failure. Let's look at the flipside of that question: How to handle success?

Jorge: Share it. Success is best when it's shared with people. I would say, "Take the blame and share the glory," knowing this is who you are. It will make you strong. When you take responsibility for what went wrong, immediately somebody steps forward to find a solution. Show that you love and you will be loved. It's the love that gets us through the hurt.

We left the table with our midsection a bit fuller as the aroma of black beans and fried food lingered around us. A certain high was reached—not drug—or food-induced but from exchanging ideas that make hope real. It was a high induced from knowing life was good and worth fighting for.

As I got into my car, I thought it had been a really good day, and everything was going to be all right.

Jorge Mursuli shortly after the passing of the
Human Rights Ordinance in 1998

PART II
THE PRACTICE OF SPIRITUAL ACTIVISM

Just as violence is a weapon, nonviolence is a weapon too.
However, the weapon of nonviolence is sharper than the
weapon of violence.
Just as the soul is stronger than the body, so too is nonviolence,
since it is the weapon of the soul, and so it is more powerful than
the weapon of the body which is made of matter.
~Imam Muhammad Shirazi

America did not invent human rights.
In a very real sense human rights invented America.
~Jimmy Carter

CHAPTER 6

How to Be a Spiritual Activist

The gap between poverty and wealth is the
main cause of our trouble.

~Archbishop Oscar Romero

Every day we live and breathe is an opportunity to make a difference and to help somebody. Like with everything else, there are right ways of making a difference, there are ways that are ineffective, and then there are ways that are blatantly wrong. Let us consider how to be a Spiritual Activist in ways that are honorable and right, no matter from which lens it is observed and analyzed.

Stand for, not against, something

All movements for change require people. If the people do not stand up and follow, it's because the message of the activist is not compatible with the people. Without public support, an activist is

107

a lone crusader. Consequently, the message needs to be examined. Is the message one that stands for something positive and tangible? Or is the person just complaining? Generally speaking, you can always find people to complain about one thing or another. There are people who are never satisfied, and your best will never be good enough. These are people who love to be heard, love to bring someone down, and love being in control. Get enough complainers in one room and a whirling pool of negative talk will suck the energy out of anyone passing by. Many Wrongful Activists are complainers. They tap into the negative energy in every community.

The challenge of every complainer is to be part of a positive solution. Some people complain because they have a legitimate problem, but how those people are moved from the negative and destructive aspect of complaining to positive action is the challenge for the Spiritual Activist. Therefore, it is important that Spiritual Activists stand for a human value that contributes to an improved wellness for all.

Let's take a look at a small group of activists who wanted to contribute humanitarian assistance to the victims of the Palestinian/Israeli conflict. The group members were moved by their humanitarian values, convinced that too many wrongs had been committed by both parties in this Middle Eastern conflict.

Case study—Palestinian/Israeli conflict: carefully choose an effort

On March 16, 2003, Rachel Corrie, a twenty-three-year-old peace activist was run over by an Israeli military armored bulldozer that was demolishing homes of Palestinians living in Gaza. Corrie was serving as a human shield, placing her body between the bulldozer and a home scheduled for demolition. The bulldozer ran over her twice. Whether or not her death was intentional is an ongoing heated debate. Zionist groups angrily accuse peace activist groups of recklessly interfering with military actions. Peace activists angrily accuse Zionists of violating the basic human rights of the Palestinian people.

Inspired by the life of Rachel Corrie and moved by her tragic death, a Mennonite church in northern Indiana made the commitment to study and discuss the Palestinian/Israeli conflict. After several months of study they were moved to action. They wrote letters to senators and other legislators, but eventually they felt their letter writing was not enough. They agreed to become involved in a humanitarian effort that promotes a peaceful solution to the conflict. With so many organizations doing work in the Middle East, the challenge of whom to support was not easy. After much discussion, the group agreed to the following criteria for organizations to meet in order to receive funding:

1. The organization and its leaders could not have any discriminatory language, be it anti-Semitic or anti-Palestinian.
2. The organization had to have a mission statement that upheld positive, universal human values such as peace, reconciliation, charity, or collaboration.
3. The organization had to be self-sustaining and the mission had to be sustainable.

4. The organization must be led and staffed by people living in the region.

Over the course of several months, the group examined the rhetoric of different organizations working this conflict. They came across a few organizations that were clearly anti-Palestinian, which they quickly scratched off the list. They found other organizations that on the surface seemed to have a balanced approach until they read statements from the leaders and found language that was bordering on anti-Semitism. These organizations were also scratched off the list.

Shortly thereafter they received a lead to look into the work of a scholar and activist, Dr. Yehuda Stolov, whose organization, Interfaith Encounter Association, seeks to foster dialogue between the Israeli and Palestinian.[29] The mission of Dr. Stolov, and the strategy employed, was compatible with the group. For several years now, the Mennonite group organizes an annual fundraiser to financially support the work of nonviolent dialogue between the Israeli and the Palestinians. This fundraising has drawn unwanted attention against them by Zionists groups. However, their strategy of promoting a positive human value helped them withstand the emotional resistance.

Build bridges, not walls

The work of justice is very difficult. It begins with the individual and then moves into the communal. The ripple effects of change must move into wider circles until entire communities around the nation or globe have felt its impact. The Spiritual Activist must open the door so that other people can participate and take the message to their communities. There is a risk when working with others that the message might be altered and the control of the movement might be lost. These risks are negligible, for every effective leader knows how to work with such factors. The bigger issue is of trust. How can trust be developed between people and communities that have never worked together before? How is trust built when other signs indicate caution?

To build trust one must be willing to believe in the goodness of people. To build trust one must let go of the pains that keep divisions strong and have faith that somehow God is working the scene. The Spiritual Activist realizes that help is needed and it may arrive from a variety of directions. Whereas the Wrongful Activist will build walls to keep other people and organizations from collaborating, the Spiritual Activist will open all possibilities for collaboration, because it is not about the activist's vision but rather the growth of the movement. Whereas the Wrongful Activist will not trust out of fear of being hurt, the Spiritual Activist knows that trust is built by extending it at the risk of getting hurt.

This was a lesson learned by Susan, an activist who seeks to help victims of domestic and sexual abuse in the migrant farm working community of Homestead, Florida. Susan Rubio-Rivera was born into a migrant farm working community and she experienced first-hand the economic and social struggles of abject poverty. She is also a survivor of domestic and sexual abuse. In 1996 she founded MUJER (Women United in Justice, Education and Reform)[30] and very quickly she became a community leader for a people that had no advocate. Her ground breaking work for

MUJER won her recognition when she was awarded the Spirit of Excellence Award from the Miami Herald (1997).

Sexual and domestic violence is prevalent in communities suffering from abject poverty and alcoholism. It is a complex issue requiring much therapy and community assistance. Every case is tragic, for they each could have been prevented if the right kind of help had been available. In the migrant farm working community, the services have been absent. To make matters worse, many migrant farm workers are undocumented immigrants and in fear of being deported. Consequently, the victims of domestic and sexual violence tend to be trapped in a perpetual nightmare of desperation, and many of them do not reach out for help. This is why the work of MUJER is so important.

The early focus of MUJER was to provide services for women and their families. MUJER was a center for women empowerment, providing mental, emotional and economic support to women who needed enough strength to walk away from an abusive relationship. This goal is much easier described than achieved. Susan learned that for the victims of domestic and sexual violence to heal they had to work with other organizations; be they clinical, law enforcement or judicial. A multi-disciplinary network of services did not exist, so Susan set out to create it. In 2004, MUJER formed the Family Violence Partnership Service Network (FVSPN), a collaboration of 10 organizations with the aim of providing comprehensive services to victims of domestic and sexual abuse.

Through the years, Susan saw that many men were also victims of domestic and sexual violence. She came to learn that the maladies of this societal disease can affect men as easily as it affects women. Consequently, she led her organization to open its doors to men. She also knew that MUJER worked best when it was in partnership with other organizations, some of which had men as leaders. The collaborative nature of Susan led her to change the focus of MUJER so that by 2011 they were reaching out to the "Men of MUJER." In October 2012, the "I AM MUJER" campaign announced a more inclusive organization and strategy. By changing the focus of MUJER, Susan was able to provide services to the whole community and increase the donations. More importantly, she helped change the conversation, so that sexual and domestic violence is no longer seen as a problem solely of women, but of all people.

Be prayerful and nonviolent

As described in chapter three, nonviolence is the signature of the Spiritual Activist. Nonviolence promotes love, change and personal transformation, whereas violence begets more violence. It seems to be common sense, but it cannot state this enough. A Spiritual Activist is nonviolent in posture, language, outlook and internal value system. To intimidate people only causes fear, not change. Nonviolence is more than just a tactical strategy; it is a way of life. Because a Spiritual Activist may be working and living in areas where violence is endemic, the question of self-defense, or defending others, has been raised often. This often leads to debating the minor difference between being a pacifist and a nonviolent activist. The general agreement is self-defense is permitted with restraint. Nonviolence is concerned with the method of how we exercise self-defense. The taking of another life, or the causing of permanent injury, is not acceptable.

For the Spiritual Activist, prayer is the daily discipline that replenishes her strength and energy required to face the challenges of nonviolent activism. Prayer is part of the daily routine, and many Spiritual Activists learn how to be in constant prayer. It is not about the words that are spoken, but about the focus. It is not about changing God's mind, but about changing yours. Prayer is the most understated, misunderstood and unappreciated aspect of Spiritual Activism. Develop the discipline of prayer and you will see that in the long run it is indispensable.

Be yourself

You don't have to become the stereotype of an activist. You don't have to change into something you are not. Express your social justice effort from the unique perspective of your individuality. When a justice effort is embraced by different members of the community, each from his own unique place, it becomes difficult for those who resist the movement to demonize it. When housewives, working men and women, elderly and young, black and white all stand up to injustice, the perpetrators of the injustice take a closer look at what is happening. When people advocate for the rights of others while remaining true to their identity and personality, other people listen because they recognize it as a genuine expression of truth.

Natalie is the grown daughter of wealthy parents. She wears expensive jewelry and fashionable clothing. She is an attractive, sexy young woman who at first glance one might mistake for a frivolous socialite. People may judge Natalie by her cover, but read a few pages into her being and you will see she is a Spiritual Activist. She is concerned about social justice and the environment and is willing to devote time to good causes. Natalie will very quickly stand up to racism, discrimination, and narrow-mindedness. She suffers no fools and knows the facts behind the issues. Because she is accepted in high society circles, she has access to many people who are not interested in justice issues. This makes her a very effective advocate. Natalie does not feel the need to camp out on the streets to become an Occupy Wall Street activist. She is comfortable with herself and seeks to make a difference in the world from within her circles of influence.

Interview: Activism Is Faith Extending Outward

Happiness is not a matter of intensity but of balance,
order, rhythm and harmony.

~Thomas Merton

The human mind is like a beautiful house with many rooms, each designated for different functions, with their own ability to store and collect information. As we grow and mature, the rooms expand. When I first met Daniella Levine at the turn of the twenty-first century, my mind was in need of expanding. Unexplored rooms in the house were being discovered. At that time, I was a junior pastor on staff who happened to pass by a meeting in the church at which Daniella was the lead facilitator. I was curious as to why a whole group of people were seated in one of the common rooms listening to this woman. The senior pastor, the Rev. Dr. Donna Schaper, saw my curiosity and motioned for me to sit next to her.

"I'm glad you're here," Donna whispered into my ear. "I want you to meet someone."

"Who? Her? Why?"

"Yes, her," she replied with a smile. "It'll be good for you. Now, shhh."

Donna had a way of bringing people together and forming connections in the community that amplified her ministerial presence. I have to credit her with several important connections in my life. She also helped me become aware of several empty rooms in my mind. The day I met Daniella, an entire wing of empty rooms was opened. A very specific awareness came to life. Daniella was then, as she is now, a maven of justice and organizational development. She spoke in a manner that inspired me to become a better pastor—not just for the wealthy people of Coral Gables but for an entire community that suffers from gross inequality.

In time, my pastoral role shifted to the justice committee of the church. This afforded me the opportunity to participate in programs that Daniella and her organization, the Human Services Coalition (now renamed Catalyst Miami), offered. We agreed to meet for the interview on the holiday of Martin Luther King Jr., a perfect touch of serendipity. Knowing she is Jewish, I opened the interview by asking her which branch of Judaism she belonged to.

Daniella: Reform Judaism is what I was raised in, and it's what I practice today. Although, I have to say, that when I was a child I did not practice Judaism. For a very long time I did not practice my faith. I started to practice Judaism about ten years ago. So it has become a recent development in my life.

Guillermo: Is there anything about your faith that falls outside of Judaism?

Daniella: Well, one of the things I love about Judaism, at least how I understand it, is that you don't really have to believe anything specific. It's a rather open-minded approach. The focus is more on how you live your life.

Guillermo: So it's not really big on doctrine.

Daniella: That's right. One of the things I've learned is that Judaism is a religion about learning. Take a look at the altar in the temple. What's on the altar? A series of books. The Torah. Everything is about the books. To my way of thinking, these books hold eternal truths. So you're asking me about my faith, and I would respond by saying that Judaism is my doorway to faith, as opposed to Judaism is my faith. Does that make sense?

Guillermo: Of course. So what happened in your life ten years ago that you approached your faith through Judaism?

Daniella [*laughter*]: My children left home. That tries anyone's faith. I guess the empty-nest syndrome did something that redirected my focus back to me.

Guillermo: But when you became an empty nester, did you crave more human interaction? What happened?

Daniella: Well, empty nesting challenged my sense of meaning. So much of our emotional and spiritual life is tied in with the care of our children. When they left, it was a shock to my sense of equilibrium. When I met Rabbi Mitch Chefitz, we were rather taken by him and his teachings. So we started to go to temple because of him.

Guillermo: Daniella, you are well-known in the community as a woman who seeks and practices social justice. How much of your social justice focus stems from your faith?

Daniella: Although Judaism is well known for having a strong social justice focus, my early Jewish education did not provide for this. As I told you, I really did not have a formal Jewish upbringing. I think my sense of social justice really came from my grandfather. He was a man of deep faith, and I guess through osmosis I picked up a lot from him.

Guillermo: Knowing you already walked that social justice walk, knowing you already had a deep understanding of how to seek and practice social justice, how did your renewal with Judaism ten years ago complement with justice?

Daniella: I know what you're asking me, but I really want to tell you about my grandfather on my mother's side, George Jaffin. As a man of deep faith he was very active in issues of social justice. He participated in many charities at hospitals, schools, art foundations, and temples. He probably gave away half his income . . . . Now, let me take this question back around to my formation. I now consider myself to be a person of great faith. I wasn't brought up to be that way, but through my grandfather's example I think the foundation was laid. I hope I'm not disappointing you.

Guillermo: No, not at all. It actually points to a long historical fact, that faith and values are more often passed down, or developed by, members of the family than through religious institutions.

Daniella: When I started to become more involved in my faith . . . I'll tell you what I learned. I learned the importance of being a person of integrity and to listen deeply to myself and others. What I got out of studying

Torah is that the focus is less about me and more about what I do with others. It's about how I show up: the small gestures, the relationships being developed. It's not about my feeling good about the program I set up that week, but more about the relationships I cultivated. It allowed me to enjoy the journey inward.

What I'm saying is . . . I went to temple to go deep, to go inward; not to go outward.

Guillermo: Because you were already out. You were already in the community doing the social justice work.

Daniella: That's right. I was already out. I didn't need more activism, nor did I want to do more. I went to temple to get away from it, even if it was just for a few hours every week.

Guillermo: So, is it fair to say that developing your faith brought you balance?

Daniella: It certainly helped me develop balance, but more so how I practice integrity. I became intentional on being present with myself and others.

Guillermo: I love it. There's something so very profound about being present, in the "here and now." Daniella, can I move this conversation to the Human Services Coalition, now called Catalyst Miami?

Daniella: Please. What do you want to know?

Guillermo: Well, can you give me a little bit of history? When did you create it?

Daniella: Seventeen years ago. As you know, my training is in law and social work. I always had the idea that

I would be involved in social justice but with a particular focus on children and families. I believe children need the benefit of a loving home, and, through support, families can be given the tools and resources necessary to provide that home. It's always been a goal of mine to strengthen families. For many years I considered the tools needed to meet that goal at the programming level and at the policy level. And I actually had a lot of great experiences in that regard. When I got out of law school I worked at the Guardian Ad Litem program, at the state legislature through the Florida Bar advocating for children. I worked in legal services representing children. So I worked a lot in areas that provide social support and programming for children and families. All that work amplified and deepened my understanding of the possibilities to make a difference.

And then welfare reform was passed during the Clinton administration, and that was a change in the way social services were delivered in this country. I was on the board for the League of Women Voters and we were looking at the impact of these policy changes. I was of the mind that the community needed to come together to provide what the government no longer wanted to offer.

I started the Human Services Coalition to meet the needs created by the changing landscape. We had two tracks. The first track was to engage people in the policy, especially those affected by these changes, so they could have a voice in the policy process. The second was to actually provide some help in navigating the system, helping them apply for services, and also planning . . .

Last year we changed the name to Catalyst Miami because we were no longer only about human services. We were doing many innovative things that point to the underlying causes of poverty and inequality in America. We've become very active in civic leadership and civic engagement and we train a lot of people in how to participate in government or community leadership.

Guillermo: Knowing you have been part of many efforts and campaigns, I would like for you to share some specific details, some nuts-and-bolts descriptions of a specific effort or campaign that you have led. How did you take the campaign from the dream to the reality?

Daniella: Well, let me see. HSC was the hub for the Community Coalition for a Living Wage, which still somewhat exists, but it was active for more than a decade. We created a coalition across various sectors. There were ten or so other ordinances being passed at the time. Ours was the first in the South, because we had cultivated fertile ground in the county commission. You know, interestingly enough, we had Cuban leadership in the county commission with a pro-labor orientation that I suppose they brought from Cuba. So, although they were all Republican Cubans, they were immediately supportive of the Living Wage ordinance, more so than the Democratic members of the commission.

Guillermo: How long ago was this?

Daniella: Wow. It's been . . . thirteen or so years.

Guillermo: So you had a dream of there being a living wage in South Florida. I suppose you had to create a task force or steering committee to get this going.

Daniella: Yes. Yes.

Guillermo: How many organizations were represented in this task force?

Daniella: There were about twenty, but five or six were most active. There was the Interfaith Committee for Worker Justice. They had a different name back then. The AFL-CIO was very active. The head of the AFL-CIO was wonderful and was able to help us view this issue from a larger social justice issue. They obviously see the larger picture: how this would help all working people, not just organized labor. Temple Israel was active. Coral Gables Congregational was active. PACT was not active at the time, but they helped us later on when Aaron Dorfman came. Legal Services was instrumental, and of course we had to get the commissioners to support it. One of the reasons it was successful is that FIU (Florida International University) has the Labor Center, and Bruce Nissen was instrumental in getting us the facts and figures needed to argue the need for the ordinance. He wrote a report to show what the costs would be if this ordinance was passed, and his report showed the costs were low and the benefits would outweigh the costs. So this campaign had a broad appeal, and many community leaders stepped up to the plate so it could it be passed. By the way, we had a huge turnout at the different county commission meetings, which was very important and very impressive to see so many people step forward.

Guillermo: From start to finish was it a one-year process or a two-year process?

Daniella: Let me see . . . probably closer to a three-year process by the time the first ordinance was passed at the county level. Then Miami Beach passed. The City of Miami passed, but Coral Gables did not pass it. We supported Broward County as they passed it a few years ago.

Guillermo: So it was a ripple effect as it moved through the different cities of South Florida.

Daniella: Right. Right. We also had staff. Bruce Jay came on as staff to help us pass the ordinance in the different localities. So it was active for about six or seven years. Maybe eight. I remember when we celebrated the ten-year anniversary of the Living Wage campaign. It's important to celebrate, because many people gave their time and effort to pass it.

Guillermo: I remember the celebration.

Daniella: If I may, I'd like to also tell you about a more recent campaign called the Penny Wise Campaign. Catalyst Miami has been playing the role of community organizer and we facilitate so that a broader community effort can arise. So we started three years ago the Penny Wise ("don't be pound foolish") Campaign for social service agencies that were at risk of losing their funding from the county. Also, we facilitated training of the constituents that receive these services so they can step forward and advocate for their own benefits. All these stakeholders are working together. At the different county commission hearings several hundred people who were united under this campaign attended and together we advocated for social services to not be cut from the budget. So now we're going on the fourth year of this campaign. And we've been successful in preventing the massive cuts.

Of course, when you talk about cutting social service you have to look at the other side of that equation—taxation. We were instrumental in the setting of the millage rate for the property taxes, the so-called rollback of the millage. There was a backlash, orchestrated by Norman Braman, who was upset at the tax increase and successfully led the recall of Mayor Alvarez and several county commissioners, including Natasha Seijas, who was the lead commissioner on the Living Wage Campaign. This backlash was about the increase in taxes, but if those taxes had not been increased those social services would have been cut.

Guillermo: Do you think the current political climate will do any harm to the progress created by these campaigns?

Daniella: Well, Carlos Gimenez, who was the mayor who followed Alvarez, surprised us all in his budget by not instituting cuts to the social services. He did cut administration by shrinking government, which will affect the whole system, including social services. But he did not directly cut the programs. So it surprised us all because we were expecting worse.

Guillermo: Wow. You never know.

Daniella: Exactly. You never know. Besides, I believe Gimenez is a pragmatic guy who knows you can't be cutting social services, especially during a downtime in the economy. On the other hand, at the state level, the legislature and governor have been slashing away at the budget. So I think this year will be the worst possible year for social services. The good news is Occupy. Occupy made it possible for people to take a look at how resources are distributed and how a huge sector of the population is not being serviced. I think some new faces will be elected who will address these issues brought forward by Occupy.

So I think the good news is that we're talking about inequality. The bad news is that budget problems we have require solutions that are . . . I think it will take a centrist like an Obama or a Gimenez to force some of those sacred cows on the table. I'm offended by the move against worker protection, but I also do understand that certain things have gotten out of control.

Guillermo: I know HSC and now Catalyst have always employed young people and created intern positions for college students. You have really made an intentional effort to include young people in your work. So if you had advice for a young, budding activist, what would it be?

Daniella: Well, something I learned from my time in the temple is the difference between charity and justice, and the journey from volunteerism to activism. I try to draw the distinction between community engagement and civic engagement. Maybe those terms aren't the perfect ones, but people mix it all up. If you go read to a child or donate at the church, is that civic engagement? I would argue not. But I believe, like Maimonides, that there is a trajectory. What we need to do is cultivate that trajectory.

You know, volunteering and donating are good things. We all need to do that regardless of where we are in the understanding of justice. But we have to help people take that deep dive into the depth of the issues and ask, "Why is this happening?" So I would say to the budding activist to ask critical questions. Take a look at where you are and seek to understand why things are happening.

Let's say there's someone asking these critical questions like Occupy. What's next? They say, "Awareness to will to action." Like any communication dissemination strategy, the first thing is to get people aware, to cultivate a curiosity. Then formulate a strategy. And that can be difficult. It can be frustrating. I mean, now they're saying corporations are people. What can you do when a corporation can donate to a political candidate and it will completely change the political process? How can we as a people do politics? So we need people to ask, "What is democracy if corporations can flood the process with money?"

So what I would say to a young activist is to ask critical questions and get started.

Guillermo: Get started from where you are.

Daniella: Let's go back to where you started. What does this have to do with faith? When I moved to Miami twenty-eight years ago, around 1983, I wasn't expecting to stay. I didn't like it here. It was a place without a sense of social justice. There were huge inequalities, without much philanthropy. I was offended. This was not a place that supported what I supported. I felt disengaged from the community. It took about ten years for me to decide that I could do something about it.

I got turned on to the idea that I could make a difference, and my journey began. Today, I feel totally different. My son said to me the other day, "Mom, you are Miami." I believe this place has changed and will continue to change. I believe Miami has the potential to show the world how it could be. It may not know how to promote civic engagement, but it's a very caring place. And that is an opportunity to change the culture. I believe we have changed the culture.

I decided at a certain point that I was going to make a difference. How was I going to tap into people's energy? What am I going to do here? Well, it's a faithful community, right? There are a lot of people going to church. There's a lot of faith in this community. Through faith, people believe they can make this world a better place. I was perplexed because they would say they wanted to change the inequalities that were all around us, but then they wouldn't do anything about it. The challenge was to take that energy they had on Sundays and push it out to the rest of the week.

Mitch Chefitz, whom I mentioned earlier, was instrumental in helping me develop a faithful integrity. I need to channel his wisdom. He said, "The test of faith is how your beliefs extend into the week, beyond the Sabbath." So if you can get to next Sunday still practicing what you believe, then you have done well.

Guillermo: That is a wonderful way of looking at your faith in action. You know, it really helps with the people who feel guilty about not practicing their faith perfectly. Most people know they live a sort of . . . discrepancy, and then organized religion throws them all sorts of guilt for that discrepancy.

Daniella: It's an asymptotic curve.

Guillermo: It's a what?

Daniella: An asymptotic curve is a line that is constantly getting closer to an axis but never quite touching it. We move in and we get a little closer to where we need to be, without ever quite getting there. I got this from one of my Torah classes. Everyone wants to reach perfection. Everyone wants to be one with God, but the proof is in the humility. If you're getting closer to God, then (*she begins to laugh*) you are not bragging about how close you are with God [*laughter*].

Guillermo: Yeah, the person who is close to God is probably nowhere near that conversation.

Daniella: That's right. It's a real dilemma. In those classes we also spoke about the persons who experience the abyss. In many ways, only those who have fallen into a chasm can know the healing power of God.

Guillermo: Well, thank you, Daniella. This has been wonderful.

Daniella: I have to thank you for coming here to ask me these questions, because I don't get the opportunity to dialogue in this manner. It really gets me thinking about what I do in a whole different light. There's one more thing I want to mention (*pointing to the recorder*). Are we still on?

Guillermo: Absolutely.

Daniella: A few years ago, Donna Schaper came to our offices and said that our office was a holy place. It was the first time I heard that, but what it says to me is that the work we do is holy. There is no doubt in my mind that the work we do is holy. But beyond that, how we are with each is also an expression of this holiness. We have to treat each other as the sacred being that we are intended to be, at the personal level and at the bigger, policy level.

As I left Daniella's home on this Martin Luther King Jr. holiday, she saw me to the car with smiles and laughter. Our time together was truly a gift for us both, for conversations of this sort are not common. For the next few days after our meeting I found myself thinking about Daniella's words. I suppose I was exploring a new room in my mind. Once again, my mind had been expanded.

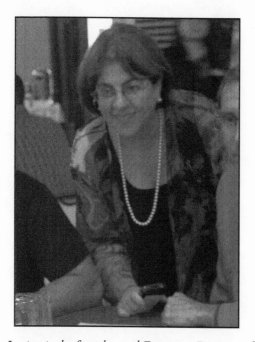

Daniella Levine is the founder and Executive Director of Catalyst Miami, formerly known as the Human Services Coalition.

CHAPTER 7

Change the World One Protest at a Time

Never doubt that a small group of thoughtful, committed citizens can change the world. Indeed, it is the only thing that ever has.

-Margaret Mead

The journey of a Spiritual Activist is one that has many twists, turns, valleys, and mountain tops. On this journey you will meet many people, face many challenges, and enjoy many blessings. Spiritual activism is an area of study, and much has been documented to assist you. You are not alone in this venture, for many people have walked this path before you. In the words of Lao Tzu, every journey begins with a single step. In the next few pages are a few.

Step 1: Identify an Injustice and Educate Yourself

Chances are you care about a multitude of issues, but it is important you focus on the one issue you can be passionate about. Because justice-work often receives little, if any, recognition choose an issue you feel passionate about. Your reward and motivation will not be monetary but in walking the path you have chosen. Once you have identified the injustice you want to work on, it is important that you educate yourself on that subject. There is a wonderful Yiddish word that I want to use: maven. A maven is a trusted expert who is wise and knowledgeable in his field. Being a maven has many benefits, but at this stage of the process it will help you get ready for the next step, which is forming a team of collaborators. People will ask you why it is important to do something about the injustice. Your knowledge on the issue will bring them on the team.

Step 2: Recruit Collaborators and Form a Core Team

You cannot work alone; all change requires collaboration. To start, you want to have to a select six to ten people who will form the Core Team that serves as strategists and decision-makers. At this stage there are only theoretical discussions about which plan of action will be more effective to reach the goal. Working with people can be challenging. Consequently, make sure that when you recruit the members of your Core Team they meet the following criteria:

1. They share common values. The Core Team needs to have a certain chemistry that makes participating enjoyable.

It is important that the members enjoy each other's company.

2. They share your passion for the justice work they are being recruited for. This will be mostly volunteer work, and often it is a thankless task. You need people who are motivated and who will be willing to be inconvenienced for the sake of the work.

3. They are willing to study the issue. The more people participate who are well-versed on the issue the better it is for everyone. Each member of the team must read, dialogue and research the issue.

4. They are willing to participate in person. Planning is best when done face to face, rather than over the phone or in an Internet chat room.

5. They are willing to disagree. There is no room for sensitive egos. Ideas need to be challenged and opposing ideas need to be presented. The work is not about any one person, it is about reaching the goal in the best possible way.

Step 3: The Planning Sessions

The planning sessions are a critical stage of justice work. Planning is what good leaders do, and good leaders know how to plan. Consequently, set up your planning sessions for success by studying the components of effective planning. Entire semester courses and degree programs are offered about planning, strategizing, and management. In this chapter and again in chapter eight, this subject is explored. Without turning this section of the book into an academic treatise, I offer the following recommendations to serve the Core Team in the beginning stages:

A. Identify reasons for planning. If the reasons for planning are not important, then the work will most likely fizzle out for lack of commitment. Agree on expected outcomes and expectations for each meeting.

B. Create language clarity. Every member of the Core Team has to agree on terms. It doesn't matter what you call certain concepts as long as everyone uses the same definition.

C. Write a mission statement. Define your goals and reasons for getting organized. The time will come to recruit people or raise money for the cause and people will want to know what they are giving to. More importantly, you have to know what success will look like at the end of the process.

D. Analyze assets and deficits, partners and obstacles. You need to spend time analyzing the many aspects of the issue. Make a list of the resources you will need. What are the internal assets and deficits? What are needs of the community? Who else is affected by this injustice? What are the partnerships you need to develop? What are the obstacles?

E. Differentiate between means (program) and ends (goal). A common error is focusing on the program and losing sight of the goal. This happens often because the programs

tend to be held in a setting where many emotional issues
are being worked out.

F. Make an action list. Another common error of many
organizations is agreeing to do something but neglecting
to assign responsibility for tasks and deadlines. A good
and thorough Action List makes clear who is accountable
for the work of the effort and can be used later as an
evaluation technique. An example of an Action List for a
sit-down protest to disrupt traffic is provided below.

ACTION LIST: Sit-down Protest Disrupting Traffic			
WHAT	**WHO**	**BY WHEN**	**NOTES**
Contact student groups, clergy, and unions	John, Mary, and Susan	November 1	Invite reps to the November 1 mtg.
Draft document with promotional info about protest	Frank, Pedro, and Maria	November 1	To be used on e-mail, blog site, Facebook, and Twitter.
Create banners and signs for the protest.	Alejandro	November 1	Bring to the Nov. 1 meeting if possible.
Research medical items needed to clean pepper spray	Oliver	October 20	Isn't water enough?
Contact news station about the protest.	Oliver	Day of protest	Need photos and video for records.

Find legal rep. to process arrests	Oliver	November 1	Contact Unions
Find a good staging area.	Oliver and Alejandro	November 1	Consider parking, green space, and proximity to US 1
Plan protest march.	Oliver and Alejandro	November 1	Create list of materials needed for protest march.
Research traffic pattern to find safest intersection.	Oliver and Alejandro	November 1	SAFETY: how many people needed to effectively stop traffic on US1
Research how to create a human chain	Maria and Pedro	November 1	Purpose is to make it difficult for police to remove protesters
Pepper Spray	Maria or Pedro	Day of protest	Train how to clean eyes

Step 4: Draft a Fundraising and Accounting Plan

Money will always be an issue. Be prepared to shoulder some financial responsibility. Without financial support your project or movement will be short-lived. Fundraising can be done in a variety of forms, but what is crucial is to have a good accounting system. Donors will want to know how the money is being used. You need to be aware that a common strategy to counter your justice effort is to attack the accounting system. If there is an organized resistance to your justice effort, they may seek your weak spot, which normally is the accounting. So a good accounting process is paramount.

Step 5: The Use of Social Media

Fortunately, activism today has a great ally with social media. Websites such as www.change.org provide for the budding activist a resource of connecting people with a justice effort. Facebook is the new communication vehicle for disseminating information. Any justice effort that is not using social media is handicapping itself. Social media can effectively grow the number of supporters into the hundreds of thousands. Make sure you have people on your Core Team who know how to manipulate the resources of social media to its fullest capacity.

Step 6: Celebrate Regardless of Success Rate

Rejoice with the people who gave of their time This is something you should budget for. Do not mix business with celebration. There will be plenty of time to call a business meeting. Laugh, dance, and sing; after all, those are the things that make life worth living.

Step 7: Evaluate

After everything is finished, it is important to step back and assess the program or effort. How, when, and who you evaluate is very important. Too often leaders want to evaluate on the site or with people who are not part of the core planning team. If possible, allow for time to reflect. There are several evaluation techniques and they require facilitation skills and the collaboration of the group. For ongoing missions or programs that require several days or weeks, it is suggested you lead a daily debriefing at the end of the day. This should be informal to serve educational and emotional purposes. An easy method is to assemble the participants in a circle and ask them to share their *high* and *low* moments for the day. For efforts that have many participants, you may want to consider breaking them up into groups of twelve with a designated facilitator for each group. Daily debriefings stimulate reflection and allow the group to share feelings and thoughts that will build community. Do not confuse daily debriefings with program evaluation. Although there is a spirit of connection between the two, an official evaluation is separate and more thorough.

Any evaluation method should examine whether the goals of the mission or effort have been met. That is the bottom line. However, often there are unintended consequences that are visible only in hindsight. To evaluate missions with a specific end date, you may want to meet with the Core Team and use SWOT (Strengths, Weaknesses, Opportunities, and Threats) as the evaluation method.[31]

SWOT analysis is a subjective assessment of data that is logically organized to assist with decision making and understanding of the issues. Strengths and Weaknesses are usually categorized as internal factors; whereas Opportunities and Threats and categorized as external factors. Evaluating with the SWOT method is usually a collective experience where members of the team offer their opinion for each category. It is important to allow for every member to participate because it is that time that the diversity of opinion may matter the most. One person's strength may be another weakness. SWOT evaluations allow for data to be placed in a 2x2 matrix where the information is connected so that a deeper evaluation can occur. SWOT evaluations have become so popular that it should be fairly easy to find materials on it.

Evaluations may create conversations that are circular in nature. One point leads to another and you may find yourself back in the beginning. To help bring clarity to the dialogue the Core Team may want to ask three questions:

1. How much work is being done to achieve the goal?
2. How well is this work being done?
3. Who is benefiting from the work?

These questions help measure the output and outcome of the program, including its tangible and observable results. Another method of evaluating is to utilize the Action List and rate the effectiveness level of each item on a scale of one to five. There should be a narrative for each item that supports the numerical assessment. This method of evaluation is often preferred over SWOT, for it is specific to each item and gives specific feedback per area.

Step 8: Plan for Growth

You have a good concept and a worthy cause. People will be supportive and will volunteer. Consequently, you need to consider your efforts over a long period of time. How do you want the movement to grow? How will you be able to grow it in sustainable ways? Often, movements lose sustainability. When planning for growth it is important to consider how to keep the Core Team and other participants interested. A proper vision and mission statement will provide the foundation for future growth. (See chapter 8 for more on mission statements)

Step 9: Pray with Your Feet

Prayer is a valued discipline in most religions. People who pray with regularity claim it helps them stay centered and confident. Activism in the faith community has a kinetic component requiring people to pray where they are and with the community they serve. Spiritual Activists make time for prayer, even when schedules are tight. Speak to most activists, and chances are they will say they are praying "with their feet." That is to say, that they do not stop for prayer. It is an ongoing process. Spiritual Activists understand that prayer is not a formula of words in a proper sentence, it is a way of life. For the enlightened individual it is a state of being.

Decision Making

At the first meeting of your Core Team it needs to be made clear how decisions will be made. This is a fundamental criteria or your effort will be short-lived and possibly create hostile feelings. Below are the three most prevalent decision-making models.

1. **Majority Rule.** Voting is required to make a decision. In many organizations, a two-thirds or 66 percent majority is required to pass the decision. In some other organizations it is 51 percent. The benefit to this method is that it is straightforward and easy. The difficulty is that it creates resentment among the losers and fosters an unhealthy environment of competition in which people lobby prior to the voting and can even be tempted to bribe or extort votes.

2. **Consensus.** Decision making by consensus usually means everyone must agree. In voting scenarios in which there are too many people, or a possibility of disruption, consensus is often redefined to be a majority of 95 percent or higher. This can be a slow process, especially in Core Teams that are diverse in opinion and values. However, it has a huge benefit because once everyone is onboard, there will be no dissent or resentment.

3. **Empowered Leader or Subcommittee.** The Core Team nominates a person or committee to study the issue and make a decision. In this model the empowered leader or committee is normally given the charge of research by interviewing stakeholders in the issue. Often, the experience and knowledge of the leader or committee provides the trust required for such empowerment.

Designating a Leader or Point Person

Having the right leader will determine the success of a justice effort. We know of several justice efforts that have failed because they had the wrong leader at the front of their cause. This has led to creating a new form of leadership where a Core Team shares the duties and responsibilities of leadership. Shared leadership promotes a horizontal structure in which consensus is paramount and no individual becomes the face of the movement. Recently, we have witnessed the use of Facebook and other social media to organize social justice movements that do not have an identified leader. Occupy Wall Street quickly grew into a movement that was too large to control, so the organizers got out of its way, allowing it to become an expression of the people. Yet most justice efforts are smaller and do not respond to social media as quickly. Having the right leadership in place can make a world of difference. In many activist groups, a leader is chosen to serve as a facilitator. Decisions are made via consensus or strong majority, and the elected leader is only a servant for the cause. This keeps people humble and allows for ownership of the cause to be shared equally.

Interview: Integrating Nonviolence

Non-violence is not a garment to be put on and off at will.
Its seat is in the heart, and it must be an inseparable part of our being.
‑Mohandas Gandhi

Nonviolence is more than just strategy. It is a thought, posture, and worldview. People who practice nonviolence on a daily basis find ways to build community, resolve matters peacefully, and extend the best they have to offer. The goal is to be more than something we practice. Nonviolence must be the air we breathe.

Arden Shank is the president and CEO of Neighborhood Housing Services of South Florida, an organization that seeks to provide affordable housing for working people of limited resources in Miami. When I first met Arden and his wife, Meribeth, it was very obvious they were not from South Florida, an area that promotes a competitive and materialistic culture. Arden is soft-spoken, pleasant, and radiates an aura of peace. Soon enough I learned they were Mennonites from the Midwest. Like a bee drawn to a new flower, I found myself frequently hovering near them, inviting them to committee work, engaging them in conversation, and listening intently to their insight.

Years ago, at a church retreat, Arden shared with me a powerful narrative about how he used the principles of nonviolence to strategize a peaceful solution to growing tensions in Goshen, Indiana, where he and his family lived for nineteen years before moving to Miami. The story made an impression and remained deep within the honeycomb of my mind. Arden gladly agreed to meet with me and share more about his nonviolence focus. We went to Garcia's, a seafood restaurant overlooking the Miami River, and after ordering a light lunch I began the interview by asking him about his religious affiliations.

Arden: I'm currently a member of the United Church of Christ at Coral Gables Congregational, but I also remain an associate member in my home church, Assembly Mennonite Church in Goshen, Indiana.

Guillermo: Were you born Mennonite?

Arden: Yes, I was born into a Mennonite family in very rural Illinois.

Guillermo: What is it about the Mennonite faith that stands out?

Arden: Well, the most significant and common aspects of the Mennonites are two things: First, Mennonites are one of three historic peace churches, along with the Church of the Brethren and the Quakers. So, peace is a fundamental tenet of ours. Over the years it has evolved from passive nonviolence to active nonviolence. And secondly, the Mennonite Church is known for its strong involvement in community and economic development projects in Latin America and around the world.

Guillermo: What formal training did you receive in the Mennonite faith?

Arden: I was a religion major in Goshen College, which is one of the main liberal arts colleges owned by the

Mennonite Church, but I also am a seminary graduate from Associated Mennonite Biblical Seminary (AMBS) in Elkhart, Indiana, and I also did one year at Wesley Seminary in Washington, DC.

Guillermo: Were you studying to be a Mennonite pastor?

Arden: (laughter) Maybe.

Guillermo: Did you have a change of heart?

Arden: I'm not sure I ever wanted to be a pastor. I started seminary with the idea of answering my own faith journey questions and to prepare for peace and justice work. By the end of seminary I knew I was not going to be a church pastor but that my work would have a justice focus.

Guillermo: How has the Mennonite faith moved you to do justice work?

Arden: In my childhood years there was always a report in church from the missionaries and a push for people to volunteer in a variety of ways. High school graduates are encouraged to do a year of voluntary service before going to college because service is central to our beliefs. Our daughter did that after high school and our son did his after college, which means they gave of their time without getting paid, without any benefits, and just focused on giving a service to the community.

For me, the driving questions were about connecting volunteer service with faith. That's why I went to AMBS. The overarching question is, "How does this fit together?" Some people go to seminary knowing they are going to be a pastor, so they take the classes to meet that goal. For me, seminary was the vehicle that helped me answer the question of why I have to work for justice. So early on I was in a systematic theology class, and although I happen to disagree with many of the principles of systematic theology, it helped me think about the questions, "Who is God and how does Jesus fit into this?"

Guillermo: That's an interesting approach. You spent more than four years trying to figure out how your faith fits into justice work and activism. Can you articulate into a short statement how your faith propels you to be an activist?

Arden: Actually, it's a little more difficult now than it would have been fifteen years ago because I have spent more time reading and listening to theologians who have completely opened up the faith issue beyond the boundaries of Christianity. Listen to Bishop John Shelby Spong and Marcus Borg, and it's obvious there's more to it than our Christian tradition has offered. But my statement would be: to me, the heart of the Christian faith has to do with a basic understanding that fair access to the world's resources is the number-one issue.

Guillermo: It's a God-given right.

Arden: Absolutely! So when we talk about the image of God, we have to understand that God is the One who provides the right to access the resources.

It's our mission to live this out. There's a hundred ways to live this mission. You don't only have to Occupy Wall Street or give all your resources to the poor. For me, the work I do with housing and economic development is my central path to live this understanding. But there's so much more. In this country, you also have to live green. We have to plant trees here and look at how we live so that we don't consume all the resources and allow others to access them.

But you know, it's not so much what I believe that matters anymore; it's what I do that matters. And that's a huge difference from where I used to be. It used to be more important to me that I know what I believe, which is why I spent so many years studying it. Now I think what matters most is what I do. What we believe doesn't matter that much. It's what we do.

Guillermo: You know, that sentence opens up a whole can of worms.

Arden: I know.

Guillermo: What little I know about the field of ethics is that it's important to know why we're making certain decisions, and that, of course, is influenced by what we believe. But I see what you're saying, because there are a lot of Bible-thumping Christians who misuse the earth's resources and promote hatred, which is clearly not part of what Christians are supposed to believe.

Arden: Yes. There's a way of questioning all this in a manner that is very instructive: "What is the difference between what we believe and what we do? Do we do what we believe?"

Guillermo: You've been trained in nonviolence. Can you share a justice effort or campaign where you had to practice the principles of nonviolence?

Arden: There are many. From 1986 to 2001, I worked for an organization in Goshen, La Casa, which provided affordable housing. In the late 1980s, Goshen's population was growing and there wasn't enough housing. So landlords were allowed to rent out housing units that were below acceptable standards . . . that were decrepit. So one of the campaigns I took on was to change the housing code for the community. Goshen was a conservative, Republican community, which meant I had to plan this campaign very carefully. And so, while we were not afraid there would be violence on the streets, the way there was during the civil rights movement, some of the principles of nonviolence still apply. In fact, we were never concerned with violence or conflict on the street. But I knew the organizing principles of Saul Alinsky, of confrontation, would not work. The nonviolent approach calls for a strategy that reduces the possibilities for verbal conflict. To have people arguing heatedly would not help the poor person who was in need of decent housing. It would only build resentment against them, and they weren't the problem.

Following the principles of nonviolence, I brought all the stakeholders into the conversation and I didn't vilify anyone. It would have been easy to accuse landlords of unethical behavior, but that would have only placed them on the defensive. Instead, I sought out landlords who were providing good, clean housing and who treated their tenants well at reasonable rents. So when we drafted the ordinance—because we had to write the ordinance that we wanted to see passed—we took it to those landlords for their review. And they said, "No problem." This ordinance was describing what they were already doing.

With their support we got ahead of the public conversation. Anyone who would oppose the ordinance would have been seen as providing lower-quality housing.

Guillermo: It would have shamed them.

Arden: And shame is a powerful tool. People don't want to lose their standing in the community. Consequently, after a year of putting this together, the ordinance was passed by a Republican leadership without opposition.

Guillermo: Let me play Devil's advocate. How much of this was principles of nonviolence and how much of it is just crafty, savvy strategic planning?

Arden: We used the basic principles of nonviolence to guide the strategic planning. The principles of nonviolence are to articulate the problem, bring the various sides of the issue together peaceably, and create the public dialogue, but we also strategized.

But your point is well-made. We didn't just sit there thinking our good intention would solve the problem, because it wouldn't have. We had to be strategic as to whom you bring together and when.

Guillermo: It sounds like a mix of common sense, faith, and wisdom.

Arden: Our organization worked mostly with people who were new to the area. Goshen was growing with poor white folks from Appalachia and with Mexican immigrants. Neither group was part of the ruling elite of Goshen. So our organization would get accused of bringing these Mexicans to town. Because we were on the forefront of this, I was often asked to speak about this issue.

One morning I was at a breakfast meeting of one of the civic clubs and a business owner was criticizing us for bringing Mexicans to town. I remember being very much aware of who was there. If you are out of step with the community you get cut off and you lose contact with the people you are guiding to move forward. So I was at that breakfast meeting and I said to that guy . . . I don't remember his name . . .

Guillermo: Let's call him Joe.

Arden: Okay. I said, "Joe, La Casa is not the entity that brings people to this community from Mexico or anywhere else. It's people like you, business owners and employers who do." I didn't have to say anymore. Everybody knew Joe employed people at very low wages in a laundry business to wash sheets in very hot and humid conditions. I didn't get any more comments like that.

Guillermo: You spoke the truth. There's nothing more powerful than the truth. Tell me about the time when you had to stand up to the KKK.

Arden: Ah yes. Well, as the non-white population grew . . . well, let me back up. Indiana is one of the strongest KKK states. I used to joke around and say Indiana was the northernmost southern state.

Guillermo: (laughs) This happened when?

Arden: From 1994 to 1998. So, as the non-white population grew in Goshen, the KKK got more forward in their activities. They would hold their KKK rallies on the streets of Goshen with frequency. Needless to say, this scared many people, but mostly the Mexicans. The police had to allow the KKK because people have a right to assemble and rally. However, local government felt they had to do something about the increased activity of the KKK. So the city council passed an "anti-mask ordinance," stating that only people with certified health problems could wear a mask in public space.

During the time for the public hearing on the ordinance, I went with the intent to speak out in public supporting the ordinance. Standing in the back of the chambers were five Klan members wearing their robes and hoods. I thought, *This is going to be interesting.* So when the time came for public comment, I got up and said my piece.

The next morning there was a note on the door of La Casa threatening us and saying they were watching us. Needless to say, our Hispanic staff found it to be very threatening. A few weeks later, the Klan announced they were going to do a rally in front of our office building. Our street was the perfect setting for a Klan rally. We were very concerned that a Klan rally, with all the hooded men, the horses, and intimidating postures they have would have a real negative consequence to our work. What were we going to do?

We did two things. The first was that we decided to receive training on nonviolent street presence to diffuse conflict. This was not sophisticated, but we felt we had to do our best to make sure nothing got out of hand. The second was to host in our parking lot a public ice cream social. We invited churches, civic organizations, neighbors, local business leaders, and anyone friendly to us. Then I met with a man who I knew was KKK but I spoke to him as if he was not part of the Klan. He knew I knew, but through the whole conversation we just pretended everything was normal. We respected the . . .

Guillermo: The charade.

Arden: Yup. Well, by the end of our meeting I had the phone number of the imperial grand wizard, who lived like an hour east of us. I called the guy and acknowledged that he and his group were going to hold a rally in front of our office building. Of course he was very surprised. I said, "We're going to have an ice cream social at the very same time you're having your rally. And the reason for my call is that we are inviting you to our ice cream social."

Guillermo: (laughter) Kill them with kindness!

Arden: Of course I knew the anti-mask ordinance was the instigator of all this, so I told him he and his group could wear their robes. "You guys want to wear your robes, fine. No problem. But you can't wear your hoods. Because our parking lot is private property, so we will not allow you on our property if you are wearing your hoods." Now, the ordinance had not passed yet and it was perfectly legal for them wear hoods. But we took a chance and told them they would not be allowed to wear their hoods.

And . . . he was completely noncommittal and very surprised I had called him. A few days before the rally was to take place they canceled it. We went ahead and had our ice cream social. More than three hundred people came and we had all kinds of people from all ages and it was a lot of fun.

Guillermo: Impressive! How many people were part of the strategizing for this?

Arden: There must be have been four to six people, senior staff mostly, and the president of the board.

Guillermo: Well, good work! There's nothing like an ice cream social to diffuse tension. You know, everything about you says peace. Your voice, posture, mannerism, and demeanor are all peaceful and nonviolent. How much of it is a genetic trait from your family, how much of it is cultural from the Mennonite community, and how much of it is intentional from your training?

Arden: A good part of it is cultural. The negative part is that there's a strong cultural tendency in the Mennonite culture to be passive-aggressive. "I don't like what you did, but I'm not going to tell you."

Guillermo: So they feel they have to agree and be pleasant at all times, even though they may disagree and be upset.

Arden: Yes, that is clearly there.

Guillermo: I've never seen you do that.

Arden: I don't do that. The newer generations of the Mennonites, especially those who come from outside the traditional Mennonite families like the African Americans and Hispanics; they don't have the passive-aggressive behavior at all. To go back to your question, some of it is definitely cultural, but some of it is my intentional strategy. In a group setting I often let the other people speak first because I want to see where everyone is at.

            Coming to Miami, this strategy paid huge dividends. As you know, I am part of a racial and cultural minority here in Miami. I was told by several Miami natives that had I come in as the middle-aged, white man from the Midwest, loud and boisterous, I would have been shut down . . . immediately. But because I listen first and speak second it created a different environment.

Guillermo: Well, the reason I bring this up is that I wonder if there is behavioral outcome from a community's commitment to peace and nonviolence. In the same manner that children today are being raised to hold postures of power and strength because of the society's value for those traits, do you think that the peaceful behavior of the Mennonite community is due to their values of peace?

Arden: I wish it were that noble. As you know from your church history, the religious ancestors of the Mennonites are the Anabaptists, and they were persecuted throughout Europe, almost to the point of extinction. The Anabaptists fled to the mountains and to the rural areas and were forced into hiding. I think that during those years of persecution they decided to be quiet, pleasant, and agreeable or else they might get their heads cut off.

Guillermo: If you were to put together a justice effort or a campaign of any sort, be it for housing, immigration, or whatever, what are some of the universal, standard steps that must be taken regardless of the differences that might exist? I realize every situation is different, but what are some of the nonnegotiable steps an activist must keep in mind for an effort?

Arden: You have to understand the situation first. When I was working the housing issue in Indiana, I often said to my employees and to the partners we collaborated with, "We have to know more about housing policy than anyone else. There can be no exceptions. And if we find someone who knows more than we do, then we have to learn from him."

Guillermo: Or hire him.

Arden: Yes, and often we would. So that's number one. You have to understand the situation and know who the stakeholders are. Number two is to bring people together. It's naïve to think you'll be able to bring everyone to the table, but at least bring some people into the effort. Collaboration and partnership will only strengthen your cause. A third one is to look for solutions. Don't just point out what's wrong. Propose a solution; otherwise, you're just a complainer.

Those are three things that have to be done, I think. You might also want to make an assessment to see what the probability is for a threat of violence. The work I do does not have to worry about violence, but in some justice campaigns there might be resistance from a portion of the community, and sometimes people resort to violence.

Guillermo: What advice would you give a young person wanting to be an activist?

Arden: Find some type of organization or church to be an activist with. Don't do this by yourself. The support of a larger group is important, especially in the early stages of activism.

Our time was running out. As with most of the activists I have interviewed, Arden had dedicated precious time to this conversation, but the other pressing concerns in his life were tugging at him. We continued to dream of a South Florida that would be fueled by a wave of activism. The question that lingered was how to light a motivating fire in people's hearts that would get them involved in justice. We parted without even attempting to tackle the question.

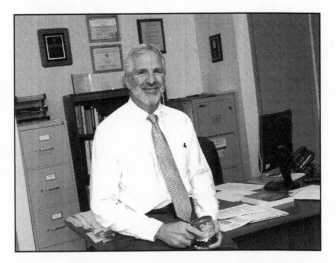

Arden Shank, Executive Director at
Neighborhood Housing Services (2012)

CHAPTER 8

Effective Planning: Two Case Studies

By failing to prepare, you are preparing to fail.

~Benjamin Franklin

A Spiritual Activist has to be prepared to answer basic questions about the work he is promoting. Whether volunteers are being recruited or money is being raised, people will want to know with whom they are dealing. This is where a mission statement is essential: Why do you exist? Who are you as an organization? Whom do you serve? A mission statement should describe the purpose of the organization. Is there an end result in mind? More importantly, how does the organization want to reach that goal?

In writing a mission statement the activist has to keep brevity in mind: less is more. If a mission statement looks like an essay, it is not a mission statement. Consider that you have to explain the purpose of your action and you only have the time allotted by a short elevator ride. This normally translates to two or three lines. A mission statement has to be clear. If a mission statement uses poetic and metaphorical language it may be confusing. Metaphors may be beautiful, but for the purposes of a mission statement they are not practical. Mission statements go straight to the goal of the effort and leave no room for misinterpretation. If your Core Team doesn't have experience in writing a mission statement, do some research and look at the mission statements of different organizations that share your values. A good mission statement is easy to find. What is difficult to find is the organization that actually does what their mission statement states. Too many organizations stray from their original purpose, and that is acceptable as long as the Core Team is cognizant of it and changes the mission statement to better reflect the work they do.

Writing a mission statement is only a first step. Project design and implementation is where the challenge truly lies. All successful justice efforts have the benefit of a strategic plan that keeps in mind the intentional stages of planning and development.

There are five macro stages in every justice effort:

- Awareness;
- Analysis;
- Relationship-building and preparation;
- Faith; and
- Action.

The Spiritual Activist knows these stages and uses them to examine what is required.

Stages in a Spiritual Justice Effort

Stage 1: Awareness

All justice efforts must begin with an awareness strategy. The activist must inform the people that a wrong is being committed and it requires action. This loud call for people to open their eyes to an injustice is a crucial first step. Once people become aware of the injustice, change becomes a possibility. As stated earlier, the need for awareness is ongoing and never fully achieved. There will always be new groups of people who need to be made aware of the injustice. There will always be people who need to be reminded why the action is required. Awareness strategies have to be integrated into every stage of the plan, for they help make the injustice known in more circles of conversation.

Consider the following resources as part of your awareness strategy:

- **The Internet and Social Media.** The Arab Spring, Occupy Wall Street, and the Joseph Kony campaign were launched on Facebook and had websites people could access. If you want to be relevant in the twenty-first century, you must utilize media and online resources.
- **Television and News Media Coverage.** Get as many news reporters aware of the injustice and persuade them to report it. This will immediately place the issue on television, Internet websites, and possibly in print. Other news agencies will pick up the article and do their own story on it.

- **Announcements in Large Group Settings.** Find places where people congregate, such as churches, temples, schools, and universities and ask for space and time to make an announcement. If approached correctly, most institutions will grant you a sliver of time and a table in their social hall for you to raise the people's awareness to the injustice. Be prepared to present your best two-to-three-minute speech and to hand out professionally prepared brochures with contact information. This is an opportunity to raise money, enlist volunteers, and promote action. Use it wisely.

- **A Team of Interacting Activists.** This is a face-to-face promotion and education of the issue. The interaction team is essential to justice efforts that need the support from the community. A common strategy of an interaction team is to canvass a neighborhood or business district. They can be protestors that hold up signs and interact with the public. They can be friendly people who are taking signatures for a petition and handing out brochures.

- **Posters and Flyers.** This should be the last leg in the communication strategy. Printing posters and flyers is expensive and consumes precious resources. However, they do promote events well. Posters and flyers should be handed out a few days before a big event. Use them as written announcements that entice people to attend the event or to go to the website and learn more.

Stage 2: Analysis

Analytical questions are raised after the awareness has been made. Who is responsible for this injustice? Who benefits? Who is affected? What is the history? What are the different groups involved? Most importantly, everyone must consider his or her role in this injustice. How can I get involved to remedy this injustice? In this stage, research is very important. All the information must be gathered, interpreted, and analyzed. It is in this stage that the activists must become mavens—know everything there is to know about this injustice until you are as familiar with it as you are with your own personal history.

Analysis tools are everywhere, and you must discern which type of analysis is needed at the different stages of your work. Below are proven analytical strategies that might be helpful in reaching a deeper understanding of the issue:

- **Study.** There is no substitute for basic research. Read as much as you can on the issue. Study your opponent's perspective to find weaknesses in his logic. Engage people in dialogue about the issue. Dialogue is important in developing the vocabulary and analogies that help promote your argument.

- **Field Research.** There are questions academic books cannot answer. Your Core Team must hit the streets and get an on-the-ground scope of the issue. Consider the following questions: Who are the different stakeholders in this issue? What is the broader community's interest in this issue? What are the resources available? Who benefits from this injustice and what is their argument? Are there any risks? Can we network with other organizations with a compatible mission statement? What do the legislators think about this matter?

- **Know Your Assets and Deficits.** Plato stressed the importance of "knowing thyself." This is an exercise of looking in the mirror as well as looking at the community. Identifying your assets and deficits will provide a picture of the road you will be facing in this justice effort. Using a flipchart, place information into two categories of either asset or deficit. The information on these columns will show where you have to concentrate your resources.

- **Create a Political Map.** It is highly likely you will have to approach government officials as part of your strategy. Know their stance on the issue. It is important to know everything else about opposing legislators. What does their district look like? How do their constituents feel about the issue? Is the legislator up for reelection? Canvass the district of key legislators and take a survey on the issue.

Stage 3: Relationships and Preparation

At this stage the activist knows an action is going to occur, but this action must not take place in a vacuum. It is during this stage of the effort that the activist must organize people and recruit them to be part of the action. To help build relationships, you might consider the following questions: What can this person/organization offer to the team? How will this person be compatible with your Core Team? What other groups of people are affected by the injustice? What is the relationship between the community and this person?

Hopefully, your Core Team is diverse and large enough that it would be less challenging to build relationships with members of the community. A lot of this is common sense, but for the sake of clarity make sure you have the following:

- Representation of the stakeholders on your Core Team. For example, if you are fighting for the rights of Haitians, make sure there are plenty of Haitians on the Core Team.
- Representation of diverse skills on the Core Team. An interdisciplinary team is more likely to create a successful strategy than one that is professionally homogenous. Regardless of how smart the team might be, we all have our blind spots and every team needs questions asked from different perspectives.
- Representation from diverse pools of resources. Everyone must bring something to the table. Some people are able to offer monetary resources. Others provide access to specific societal groups, and others represent their organization and the resources of that organization.

Stage 4: Faith

The internal fortitude to step forward and take action often stems from our faith. One of the principles of nonviolence is the belief that justice will prevail. That is a statement of faith. We must have faith that our actions matter and that justice will be attained. We must have courage to stand against the forces of oppression and know that God is calling us to do so. The person who allows for fear to dictate his actions will avoid the confrontation at all cost. Avoidance is not a mark of the Spiritual Activist. Before we are to step forward into action, we first stand on our faith. Often we are not sure of what will happen to us for stepping forward. We might be ridiculed, arrested, or peppered sprayed. It is faith that provides the foundation upon which we take a stand.

As people of faith, there are several internal action items we utilize.

- We pray. To be prayerful before, during, and after a justice action provides that inner confidence that makes all Spiritual Activists remain cool in the face of conflict.
- We have higher expectation of conduct. We are leading by example in every way. The moral principles of our faith keep us above the fray, knowing we must be people of integrity, fully aware that the means is as important as the goal.
- We rely on a positive, inclusive, and relevant interpretation of the Holy Scriptures. Instead of a literal understanding of the sacred writings, we seek to find God's guidance in a manner that is consistent with our postmodern society.
- We know we are part of something larger than ourselves. The effort is about a larger vision for a larger community that is made up of all God's children.

Stage 5: Action

Before the action is to happen, the Spiritual Activist must have a clear answer to the following questions: What is the goal of the action? What is required of me? Who will benefit from the action? During the action, the Spiritual Activists must be mindful of the principles of nonviolence in the same manner that a football player is of his helmet, a meditating yogi of her mantra, or a writer of his pen. During the action the activists must be in complete control of their words, actions and reactions. The other people in the scenario might be "out of control," reacting negatively to this action, making it all the more important for the Spiritual Activist to practice the spiritual disciplines of nonviolence and peace. It is in this moment that she will be distinguished from the rest.

Let us now look at two environmental justice efforts—one that succeeded and one that failed. Both addressed issues of environmental justice, but they had very different outcomes due to their differences in planning and community organizing. Why a program succeeds is important to study. Equally important is knowing why a program fails. The success and failure of a justice effort reaches beyond the effort itself. Like ripples on a pond, the success or failure of an effort will extend into the activist's sense of self-worth and general outlook on life. Activists who experience success are more likely to take on other efforts, while activists who experience failure are more likely to develop a limited outlook that will inhibit future activism. Consequently, every activist has to take the volunteers' time very seriously. These people are giving more than themselves; they are building the foundation on which future activism will stand.

Case Study: Arthur and the Voter Registration Drive

From 2002 to 2004 Kirk Arthur worked as a community organizer for an asthma eradication program in the Latino community of East San Diego in Southern California. The health department had provided statistics that more than sixty percent of the children in that region suffered from asthma. Because asthma is often caused and triggered by environmental conditions, the program set out to tackle this crisis using three strategies: medical intervention, asthma education, and community development. It was the third strategy that employed Arthur, a man who had lived in Central and South America and understood the mindset and culture of Latino immigrants living in poverty.

The asthma crisis in East San Diego was triggered by poor housing conditions. Most of these residents lived in rental apartments that suffered from a rat and cockroach infestation. It is a medical fact that cockroach debris and rodent droppings are a trigger for asthma attacks. The residents complained with vivid stories of rodents and insects crawling over the children, yet little was done to correct the problem. The zoning laws of San Diego did not consider rental buildings as residential but rather as businesses. Residential zoning was designated for neighborhoods that had the standard three-bedroom homes with a backyard. This zoning interpretation favored the landlords and not the residents. Consequently, the residents of East San Diego had little recourse in the court system to improve their living conditions. Meanwhile, the children of the immigrant Latino families were having difficulty breathing. If the asthma crisis had any chance of being eradicated, it needed the guidance of an activist and community organizer.

Arthur realized early on in the process that a contributing factor to the problem was the self-limiting view of the residents. Illegal immigrants tend to develop a survival mechanism of invisibility, which becomes integrated into every aspect of their lives and is then handed down to their children. Nobody stands up for their rights in fear of being deported. The invisibility mode remains with them even after they become citizens and are legal. In an effort to remain hidden, they did not register to vote nor did they participate in any civic function. After many conversations with the residents of East San Diego, Arthur and his Core Team wrote a simple mission statement that guided their strategy:

To educate the people of East San Diego about the benefits of voter registration and to register 85 percent of the qualified residents using health and community development as the motivating tool for voter registration.

This mission statement emphasized the need for education on the benefits of participating in the political process. This may seem like a no-brainer, but as Arthur learned, it was very challenging. With the help of neighborhood churches and business leaders, Arthur and his team led a series of meetings, at which the people complained about the slum-like conditions, the gang violence, and the unemployment. After listing the complaints, Arthur focused on the one complaint that was most pressing: the health of the children as threatened by the overabundance of cockroaches and rats. It didn't take long to make the connection between the cockroaches and the overflowing garbage bins that were emptied only once a week by the sanitation department. Many of the East San Diego residents worked in wealthy neighborhoods and knew garbage was collected twice a week throughout the city. Arthur asked why they thought the city collected garbage in their neighborhood only once a week. The people cried discrimination.

He nodded and agreed but added that there was a bigger reason. "You're invisible to them," Arthur said matter-of-factly. "They don't see you because you don't vote. Politicians only see those people who vote. Register to vote and you will see that within a year we'll have the sanitation department picking up your garbage twice a week. And then you will see how the cockroach and rat population in your neighborhood will diminish, and your children's health will improve."

Arthur got 88 percent voter registration from that neighborhood. He mobilized protest marches and sit-ins to get the media coverage needed to shame the politicians into action. Within months, politicians from both parties were visiting the residents and listening to their complaints. Within the year, the garbage was picked up twice a week. This success eventually led to other community development projects in East San Diego, all of which were a direct benefit of Arthur's voter registration drive.

Arthur's mission statement kept the effort focused. East San Diego had such a wide spectrum of troubles that it would have been easy to have been distracted by the "discrimination" energy, but because he knew his goal, he directed his speech and his behavior toward it.

If we examine the mission statement once more we can see the two basic components: purpose and method. Arthur's purpose was to get 85 percent of the qualifying residents in East San Diego to register to vote. The method to reach the goal was to link the desperate need for community development to the political process. Brilliant! But the success of this effort extended beyond the mission statement. A series of right steps were taken.

Right Step #1—Community Knowledge

Arthur knew the community. He invested time to build trust. This does not come easily for everyone. It did help that Arthur spoke Spanish, and he found ways to connect culturally in order to build trust. Knowing what the community needed, their aches and pains, was priceless in achieving the goal.

Right Step #2—Proper Strategy

Arthur took the time to strategize with a Core Team about how the goal could best be achieved. Voter registration is a touchy subject. The people living in this community viewed the political process with suspicion. In his strategy, Arthur offered voter registration late in the process and only as a solution to their problems, not as a civic duty. Like a chess game, Arthur and his team were intentional in their strategy.

Right Step #3—Follow Through

Arthur did not walk away from the community after the voter registration. He made sure the politicians came to visit and saw the overflowing garbage and the invasion of cockroaches. He followed through to make sure the political process would yield the tangible benefit of a second garbage pick-up.

Right Step #4—Understanding the Bottom Line

Ultimately, Arthur understood the voter registration drive was not about politics. It was about integrating a marginalized community with the larger. It was about the health of the children and people breathing good air. It was about improving the quality of life.

Not every effort is as well thought out and executed as Arthur's. Let us examine another worthy effort that failed even though it was well-intentioned.

Case Study: Canopy over Miami [32]

In the late night hours of August 24, 1992, Hurricane Andrew swept through South Florida, flattening entire neighborhoods and displacing many residents. Throughout most of the region, trees were uprooted and snapped in half. After the hurricane, neighborhoods that enjoyed the shade of full-grown trees were now completely exposed to the hot South Florida sun. By 1997 only a small percentage of the trees lost in the hurricane had been replaced. Later that fall, a small group of college students decided to plant trees throughout many neighborhoods in South Florida. Several of these students had parents in local government, and they knew they could enlist their help. Canopy over Miami became a student-driven and student-led effort to restore the ecosystem of South Florida with trees that could withstand hurricane force winds.

Their mission statement was, *Canopy over Miami, with the collaboration and funding of local government, seeks to plant a thousand trees in the area of Cutler Ridge and to educate homeowners about the importance of caring for them.*

One of the parents, who wanted to see his daughter's project succeed, found five thousand dollars from charitable organizations interested in environmental restoration projects. Canopy over Miami now had a budget. By November 1997 the students had purchased seventy-five saplings at a reduced price and were planting them with enthusiasm. They wrote and printed documents to promote Canopy over Miami and to educate residents on how to care for trees. They collaborated with local churches to recruit volunteers for the tree planting labor. Every Saturday for eight to ten weeks, these students planted trees in people's yards and felt good about the work they were doing. Not one of them realized the residents felt differently.

By January 1998 seventy-five trees had been planted and more than a thousand hours had been given by the team and volunteers. Approximately thirty-eight hundred dollars had been disbursed toward the project. Considering that most organizations have budgets in the millions of dollars, this amount of money is minimal and demonstrates good administrative skills.

Despite such good financial managements, some serious mistakes were committed that led to the demise of the project. By March only twenty-eight trees remained, of which eleven seemed to be in critical need of care. A year later, there were fourteen trees remaining and the project was closed. Canopy over Miami had an 18 percent success rate. What went wrong? Is there anything that could have been prevented? Let us learn from their mistakes.

Wrong Step #1—Language

The students committed a common mistake in assuming the English language was the primary language of the community. They thought the residents would understand their mission without the need for dialogue. The main reason this dialogue did not occur was due to a language gap. The students were primarily English-speaking, whereas the residents spoke either Spanish or Creole. The students approached each resident with an official-looking letter written in English. This letter created anxiety and intimidation in the residents. They did not understand what the students were doing and they were afraid to ask. Not wanting to create a problem, the residents allowed the students to plant the saplings on their property without fully understanding the project or how to care for these saplings. Consequently, these unwanted trees soon died.

Wrong Step #2—Cultural Ignorance

Many of the Caribbean residents come from an island culture that retains agricultural values. They have an affinity for fruits such as mango, avocado, and guava. Had they been presented with a fruit tree, the chances of the residents caring for the trees would have increased exponentially. Instead, the college students offered them oak trees. In general, Caribbean people view the oak tree as a leaf shedder. It doesn't flower or bear fruit. Why would they care for a tree whose only contribution is to drop leaves?

Wrong Step #3—Ownership

Many of the residents were not the homeowners. They were simply renting, and that distinction was never a factor in the strategy. A family that rents does not have the same level of care for the property as a family that owns. Consequently, the students soon learned that most of the trees they had planted were not being watered. Also, residents did not have to pay a single dollar for the tree. They did nothing to claim it as their own. People who do not own the idea will not work toward it. The residents had no ownership over the effort, the property, or the trees.

Wrong Step #4—We Know Better

Often it is not the truth that prevails but the perception of the truth. In this case of Canopy over Miami, there was a cultural tension that needed to be addressed. This tension is not a reflection of the students but of society as a whole. It is tension between insider and outsider, us and them, light skin and dark skin. It seems that the students, for the most part, were ignorant of this tension. They came to the residents offering a gift, but the residents saw an insult. What matters is not what the students said but what the residents heard. One of the complaints was, "Who do they think they are telling me I should plant a tree? Is my house not good enough for you?"

Wrong Step #5—Moving Too Fast

The students were in a hurry. They skipped over crucial strategic steps in order to get the trees planted, which led to the eventual death of 82 percent of their trees. Had they moved more slowly, collaborating with the residents and local leaders, they would have increased their success ratio. It takes time for people to consider why a tree is important. It takes time for people to develop the trust needed to accept a tree and the responsibility of caring for it. It takes time to strategize, to plan, and to include people in the process. It takes time to build relationships. Slower is better, especially when the participation of a community is needed.

Wrong Step #6—Not Understanding the Bottom Line

The saddest part of this failed environmental effort is that the students unknowingly contributed toward wrongful activism. The pain and frustration of the failure had lasting negative impacts on the students' future civic engagement, on the residents' understanding of environmental justice, and on the volunteers who gave of their time for an effort that was mismanaged. Ultimately, it's not about the trees. It's about looking out your front window to see the shade and beauty of a tree, the birds nesting in it, and the knowledge that life is good. It's about improving the quality of life.

Empowering the Community

The communities in San Diego and Miami had environmental issues that required broader assistance. Although they had different environmental concerns, they both offer a lesson about the importance of empowering the community. The effort led by Arthur in San Diego focused on changing the departmental budget and policies for a community that was not being served. In this effort, it was necessary for the community members to demand changes in the sanitation services in order to achieve a degree of environmental justice.

In the Miami effort the community members were never organized and included in the process. It was obvious to the students that trees were required in order to restore the environment, but the community members were never empowered to ask for the trees. The success and failure of these respective efforts all depended upon the involvement of the community members. Regardless of how justified an effort might be, if the residents are not part of it, it is bound to fail.

CHAPTER 9

Education:
The Mighty Sword of Activism

The pen is mightier than the sword.

~Edward Bulwer-Lytton

There was a time, not too long ago, when the word "nigger" was said openly by Anglo people who were part of the dominant culture. This word was meant as an insult and was offensive to African Americans. We are indebted to the many Spiritual Activists who fought and died for this injustice to be addressed and corrected. This injustice was part of a larger societal illness with a long history of oppression and economic inequality. Just as an onion is peeled one layer at a time, the many offensive layers behind the word "nigger" needed to be addressed one step at a time. Over the course of several decades people from all walks of life sought to educate the public about racism and how to confront it. Today, in the year 2012, this word is no longer accepted, and those who choose to say it know someone will call them on it.

I am proud to know that a new generation is being raised with higher ideals. I am proud to witness the many interracial couples that are accepted and embraced as the norm. It is a testament to how far we have come as a society. I am confident the day will come when Americans of different races will live and love in harmony without fear of discrimination or facing an ugly, racist slur. In certain pockets of the nation, that day has arrived. Sadly, in other regions that day is still a distant dream. Consequently, the work of educating all people in every community across the land needs to persist until discrimination of any sort is no longer accepted in any circle of society.

The Importance of Being Educated

Spiritual activism always begins with education and remains a central strategy. Every encounter is an opportunity to educate. Spiritual Activists educate the public not only with words but with their behavior and life choices. What a person eats, wears, and purchases is often a louder statement than what he says. The Spiritual Activist must be ready to confront a wrongful statement in order to educate whoever is listening. The duty of educating the people is ongoing, for we know laws can be repealed and wrongful thoughts can once again find their way into the mainstream.

As we educate people on justice issues, we must keep in mind the following basic lessons that are recurring from generation to generation:

1. The difference between charity and justice
2. How to identify labor injustices
3. How to network and collaborate
4. Diversity and multicultural training
5. Historical lessons on sexism, racism, homophobia, and religious persecution
6. How to use the political process for justice effort
7. How to live a nonviolent life and be a peaceful activist
8. How to identify and stop violence, be it domestic or otherwise
9. The sacredness of life
10. The sacredness of the earth and its resources
11. The importance of dialogue
12. How to organize people for a justice effort

One of the less costly forms of education is a facilitated dialogue. In many schools across the United States, school counselors facilitate dialogue groups with the students about a variety of issues: race, gender, sex, sexuality, bullying, violence, drug use, teen pregnancy, etc. These dialogues help raise awareness with the hope of eliminating the injustice in the next generations. A good facilitator will combine the dialogue with exercises that are designed to shift the view point of the participants.

After the assassination of Rev. Dr. Martin Luther King Jr. in 1968, Jane Elliot, an elementary school teacher in rural Iowa, led her grade school children in an exercise and facilitated dialogue about discrimination and racism. The "blue eye/brown eye" exercise was designed for children in a homogenous community to experience discrimination based on biological differences of eye color.[33] On day one of the exercise, Elliot told her students that blue-eyed children were superior to those who are brown-eyed. On day two, she turned the tables and said that brown-eyed children were superior. She then led the children through a dialogue and a written exercise. Her two-day lesson was published and Elliot soon after developed a diversity curriculum that created a new educational paradigm, connecting justice with education.

Education, through the course of many years, will change the mindset and culture of entire communities to allow for a just and fair approach. But education alone is not the answer. Education alone will not create a just and fair world. The power of greed is too strong. As Spiritual Activists strategize a plan to overcome an injustice, they must be intentional about moving their efforts through the different stages that will lead to an effective and successful action.

Interview: Higher Purpose and Higher Meaning

Only one who devotes himself to a cause
with his whole strength and soul can be a true master.
For this reason mastery demands all of a person.

~Albert Einstein

David Lawrence Jr. is possibly the best-known advocate for children's rights in the state of Florida. He is a man of great intellect, eloquence, and accomplishments, but his greatest achievement was his dual campaign in 2002 and again in 2008 to pass a ballot measure in Miami-Dade County known as The Children's Trust. At a time when people were demanding a decrease in property taxes, David Lawrence was able to lead a movement that placed the needs of children as a high priority for Miamians. He followed this landmark win with a statewide campaign, The Children's Movement, to make all children the first priority of Florida's legislature.

Needless to say, David Lawrence is a very busy man, with many people demanding a slice of his time. That he would agree to meet with me is not uncharacteristic of him, for he often tries to make everyone feel as important as any CEO or state legislator.

David is a delightful man whose skills as an orator surpass those of any politician or preacher. As a recognizable leader in the community he is always in great demand as a speaker. Through the years he has befriended the various senior pastors of my church and accepted their invitation to speak from the pulpit. As a young associate pastor, I thought I was invisible to him, but to my surprise he took notice of me and knew of my family history in Cuba, an impressive feat since most Anglo Americans know little, if any, Cuban history. I have always found David to be approachable, gracious, and affable. Yet as the interview date neared, I found myself getting nervous.

The thought that I was going to interview David Lawrence, a man who can go toe-to-toe with any Ivy League scholar; who has won multiple journalism awards; who was editor and publisher of several newspapers such as the *Miami Herald*; and who has national, if not global, recognition began to intimidate me. To make matters worse, on the morning of the interview I woke with a splitting headache. During the previous night I'd made several unwanted trips to the bathroom and was suffering from what I surmised was a mild case of food poisoning. As I stared at my ashen complexion in the mirror, I convinced myself I was not as sick as I looked. I had about three hours before the interview— more than enough time to clean up. Just in case, I took eight hundred mg of ibuprofen and began a cleansing regimen of lemon water and chamomile tea. Without a doubt, vomiting on David Lawrence was not an option.

I met him at his office, on time and with my best smile. I was not sure for how long I could keep my insides from exploding, but I realized his time constraints would play in my favor. This was a test of intestinal fortitude I was determined to pass.

Guillermo: Dave, I know you have time constraints, so if you like we can jump over to question number four.

David: Why don't we begin at the beginning?

Guillermo: Okay. I would love to hear about your origins.

David: I'm from New York, born into a large family. I was baptized in St. Patrick's Cathedral. My parents were romantics, in every sense of the word. My father was a newspaper man in the old *New York Sun* at the start of the 1940s. My parents decided the best place to raise children would be on a farm. So I grew up on a farm, a chicken farm. There were other animals there, but poultry was the main source of revenue. This was in upstate New York, on the heel of Lake Ontario, where the snow comes off the lake and snowdrifts can be taller than the house. We lived on this chicken farm from when I was six until I was fourteen. Ultimately the farm was in danger of failing. My father came from a strong Irish-Catholic family. My mother came from an Episcopal family, and she converted to Catholicism. We went to church every Sunday. We clearly understood the difference between a venal sin and a mortal sin. So I grew up in a home where about eight o'clock every night everybody knelt down to say their prayers.

Guillermo: How many siblings did you have?

David: Eight, seven of whom are still living. We left the farm and we moved to the west coast of Florida. We lived in a town named Oneco, which is a really small town. I graduated from high school in 1960. It was a very different time. I went to an all-white school. The sheriff of my county, Manatee County, led the Ku Klux Klan through the streets of black East Bradenton.

When I went to the University of Florida it was an all-white university, but it was desegregated in my third year. So it was very much a time of ferment. I met and fell in love with my wife when we were working on the college newspaper. We've been married for more than forty-eight years. My wife is Jewish. We were married in the Catholic church at a time when you had to promise to raise the children as Catholics—although my children always had a sense of Judaism. My wife is a member of Temple Judea. They do very good work and I have the utmost respect for the two rabbis there.

What's more important than any of that is that I grew up in a home with an extraordinary set of values. My father would sit us down at the dinner table and quiz us on history, current events, and government. We were expected to read the newspaper, to read books, and to make something of ourselves. And woe be unto you if you didn't know the name of the governor.

I feel blessed. I am blessed. I had a great childhood. I'm a very satisfied man with my home and my work. In my thirty-five years of working in the newspaper business I never missed a day of work. Obviously, I had my vacations and days off, but I always loved my work. How many people can say they interviewed Fidel Castro, Alberto Fujimori, and had dinner with the queen of England?

Guillermo: Do you see any connection between the spiritual message you hear on Sunday mornings and your work Monday through Friday?

David: Don't get me in trouble, now . . . . Too often I have not been stirred by Catholic sermons. I prefer storytelling, wisdom, and commentaries on issues of our time. So at least half a dozen times a year I will be in a black church on Sunday, and my wife and I will be the only white folks there. I do attend Friday night temple services with some frequency. I recently attended a mosque for the first time in my life. If you are Catholic—did you grow up Catholic?

Guillermo: Yes, sir.

David: Well then, you know that if you're Catholic you don't really read the Bible. Things may have changed over time, but at least in my era I never learned directly from the Bible. We instead learned from short biblical excerpts from the gospels and epistles. I love going to your church because it is joyful and lively and the sermons are relevant. I love the music and you all indulge me by singing all four verses of the . . .

Guillermo: (laughter) "The Battle Hymn of the Republic."

David: (smiling) That's a wonderful hymn. In black churches, music is hugely more important. And I have gone on a number of occasions to Victor Curry's church, where the service will last more than two-and-a-half hours, and I don't feel the passage of time.

Guillermo: So does your understanding of God extend beyond what you have experienced in church?

David: Oh, very much so. It seems quite accidental that I was born a Catholic. I do not believe God plans our lives down to those details, but I think it is crucial that we all have a sense of a higher being and a higher purpose. When a person experiences loss, our very existence is questioned. Having lost my parents, experienced several miscarriages through our daughters, and having our son-in-law choke to death, I need to believe there is something beyond what I am doing today. I need to believe there is some higher purpose behind all we are supposed to be striving for. It's crucial. I need to believe in something greater than what I am involved in.

Guillermo: The formation and success of The Children's Trust has placed you as among those who has worked for justice and seen its positive impact. Do you connect your sense of justice to your faith?

David: I do. I genuinely believe I am in God's world and I need to do God's work. Listen, I am blessed with never having been a cynic. I always thought there was some higher purpose in life. I love that quotation from George Bernard Shaw about burning the candle at both ends: "At the end of my life I want to be thoroughly used up." I'm not saving my energy for the afterlife.

Guillermo: Can you tell me about your campaign, The Children's Trust?

David: In 1996 the governor of Florida, Lawton Chiles, set up a commission on education to prepare Florida for the next millennium. I was asked to chair one of the task forces, the one on school readiness. This set me on a whole new path. I actually hesitated to be part of that commission because I thought it might be politicized. But Lt. Gov. Buddy McKay called me and told me I needed to be part of it. Reluctantly I agreed. So in 1998 I decided to retire, but the part of the story I normally don't share is that at the same time this was occurring, (American media company) Knight Ridder wanted to make *The Herald* more profitable. Tony Ridder wanted to raise its operating margin from 18 percent to 25. I said to him, "I don't think I can do this." They asked me to look into it and I did. It required laying off 185 people. I decided I had worked too hard to get the paper where it was and I was just tired of laying people off. I didn't want to cut any more jobs.

When corporations wonder why American workers often have little loyalty, frequently it's because corporations don't deserve loyalty. I just refused in my soul to lay off anybody else. So I announced my retirement. Incidentally, they have laid off hundreds more than the 185. When I went to *The Herald* in 1989 we had 2,600 employees. They have just about

700 now. That should give you a sense of how things are being run.

Anyway, a few days after the announcement of my retirement, a man by the name of Jerry Katcher called from Aspen, Colorado. Now, I didn't know Jerry Katcher that well. I knew he owned a bank. We were acquainted with each other, but I didn't know him well. I had invited him once to a holiday gathering at my home back in 1990 or '91, maybe '92. (My wife) Bobbi and I do this every other year. We find 150 people and gather them in the backyard, over by the swimming pool. Orlando Bosch, the convicted terrorist, was there one year. I had the archbishop there and Bob Graham and many other people.

Well, Jerry Katcher was there that year and he called me the following day. He said, "That's quite a gathering of interesting people you had last night. I'm the chair of the nominating committee for the (New World) Symphony and we're always talking about having minorities on the board. Do you have any recommendations?" So I told him I'd think about it, and by the next day I sent him about fifty names with addresses and phone numbers of people I thought would be good candidates. He never forgot that. So when my retirement announcement went out on a Tuesday, that Saturday he called me at my home. He said, "We don't want you to leave town. If you want to work for the future of children, (my wife) Jane and I will set up a foundation." And that's how it started. It was just out of heaven. The Katchers are heroes of my life. This chapter of my life wouldn't have happened without them.

The following year I spent five months learning everything I possibly could about this issue. In order for me to do my work, I needed to have an intellectual underpinning. I needed to see a higher purpose in all this. So I went to France to see the Western world's foremost integrated system of early childhood learning. And then I went to Sweden to learn their system of home visiting and other concepts. Out of that came a decision to try to do a dedicated funding source for children. It had been tried in 1988 by Janet Reno and others, but it failed. In my soul I knew we had to try this again, but first we needed to build a movement for all children. If I am going to try something, I don't like to be unsuccessful. I can talk a good game, but talk doesn't mean much if you don't make a difference.

When we wrote the ordinance in 2003 we put in a five-year sunset (a clause that brings the ordinance to pre-determined end) in order to better pass it through the commissioners. Well, as you know, in 2008 the economy was failing and we were still able to pass it for a second time with 85.4 percent of the votes.

Guillermo: Well, our time is almost up, and I want to ask you a few more questions, if you don't mind. You've been successful in building a bipartisan movement. The importance of that is obvious. But please tell me how the current political climate contributes to the bipartisan nature of your work.

David: My naiveté is a studied naiveté. So much of the world is about relationships and building relationships. I have been a registered independent for more than twenty years. I work hard at maintaining relationships with people, including people I would never vote for. I meet with an extraordinary number of people. I don't meet with them to further a political agenda but rather to build a relationship. I need to build the kind of credibility that would get people to realize it just makes sense. I'll give you an example.

A lot of people in power might say, "Boy, have we made progress in education!" And I would say, "Nationally, three out of every four seventeen-year-olds cannot enter the American military because they have a substance abuse problem, or a criminal problem, or an academic problem, or a physical problem." Wow! When I went to high school we were number one in the world for graduation rates. We are now twenty-first. When I went to college we were number one in the world for college graduation rates. We are now sixteenth. Twenty-eight percent of fourth graders in the state of Florida cannot read at minimally proficient levels. Sixty-one percent of tenth graders cannot read at grade level. Ouch! What a recipe this is for a very different world, in which we will be significantly less competitive. The only answer is to get more people educated, and not because this is a nice thing to do but because this is the best contribution for the community and country.

Guillermo: It is refreshing to hear that building relationships is such an integral part of your activism. This past year we saw a lot of demonizing in the news: Tea Partiers and Occupiers alike demonizing people and each other. What advice would you give a person who is looking to begin a justice effort of advocacy or activism?

David: Well, I spend an enormous amount of time talking to people who are not in power. There's this woman who is an educator who sends me Bible verses everyday. I am always learning something from her. I never want to eat alone. I'm always having lunch or breakfast with someone who can stimulate my thoughts, or give me an opportunity to stimulate theirs. All this is to say I am always meeting with people, aware that there is a higher being guiding us, and possibly I am supposed to meet with these people for a higher purpose. I wouldn't know how to do what I do without the awareness of a higher being and a higher purpose.

So, my advice to a budding activist would be to build relationships and to become a voracious reader.

Guillermo: (nodding) And . . .

David: I would hold as an example that I push people to be constantly aware of who is around them and to know about what is happening in our community and world. You shouldn't work for me if you don't read the newspaper every day and books regularly. Because how are you going to be of use to anyone if, when the opportunity to make a difference arrives, all you can do is recount the video game you played the night before? I read two newspapers every morning, the *New York Times* and the *Herald*, because I don't want to go around without an idea of what's going on, and so forth. It frightens me people think they are informed because they receive headline news on their BlackBerry. They think, somehow, they are informed citizens.

The conversation continued, and we were way past the allotted time. Dave Lawrence didn't seem to mind, and I had forgotten that my insides needed relief. We were both energized by the conversation when Dave decided I should meet a member of his staff. With a twinkle in his eye, he called out his name.

David: I want you to meet Vance Aloupis. Hey, Vance, got a minute?
Vance: (entering) Yes?

Vance is young, younger thirty, slim and handsome with an intelligent countenance. More importantly, he has the kind of vibrant energy hopeful people carry. His smile is genuine as we exchange pleasant introductions.

David: Tell Guillermo what your first interview with me was like.

Vance: Terrifying. (laughter) We spent two-and-a-half hours at Coral Bagels. It was eye-opening because, for me at least, you think you know something but then you realize you're just skimming the surface.

David: You've been here for a year and a half now. What have you subsequently learned?

Vance: In general?

David: Yes.

Vance: This is being taped?

David: Don't worry about that. You're among friends, and you can trust Guillermo. I do. So just relax and tell us what have you learned about yourself and your life here.

Vance: I'm realizing what it means to manage people and to be a leader. I haven't been in the workforce that long because I just graduated from law school, but I have worked for very few people. I think the expectations Dave sets allow me to be a better person. He's tough, but again, the ability to inspire and encourage people is very important. I learned in the first two hours with Dave that I didn't know nearly what I thought I did. That's an important realization to make, especially for people of my generation. We get information very quickly and we focus on specific . . . blurbs. I have learned how to be a more rounded person.

Dave: Now you're a highly principled person. You attend church regularly and you have a family. I happen to

know you are highly spiritual and ethical. What can
you say about the work we do and your value system?

Vance: Well I come across a lot of good people, but around
here Dave raises the bar, and it's not just about being
an average good person. It's about making a difference
and putting our values into work, into action.

David: Vance is one whose potential I see no end to. He works
very hard—not as hard as I do, but he tries to keep up.

We all laughed and exchanged genuine appreciation for each
other. David walked me to the elevator and I noticed, once again,
a radiant bliss in his energy. He smiles with his whole face and
that smile is an extension of his soul. I think if there's anyone who
has found a key to happiness, it's David Lawrence. He told me
during the interview he has a higher purpose.

David Lawrence, reading with school children in 2008
after the passing of the ballot measure for the Children's Trust

CHAPTER 10

Rise of the Wrongful Politician and the Wrongful Policy

We here highly resolve that these dead shall not have died in vain,
that this nation, under God, shall have a new birth of freedom;
and that government of the people, by the people, for the people,
shall not perish from the earth.

~Abraham Lincoln (1809-1865)

On December 17, 2010, Mohamed Bouazizi doused himself with gasoline and set himself on fire in the ultimate act of protest against the corrupt and violent government of Tunisia. Bouazizi, age twenty-six, lived in abject poverty with his family in the town of Sidi Bouzid, where he sold fruits and vegetables from a pushcart. After years of being harassed by the local police, Bouazizi complained to a local government official, Ms. Faida Hamdi, who not only refused to hear his case but humiliated him in public. Within an hour, Bouazizi knelt in front of the government building with a gasoline container. He yelled, "How do you expect me to make a living?" and set himself on fire. Officials ran to his aid and poured water on him, which only worsened the situation. Eventually, they managed to put out the fire. He died eighteen days later. Bouazizi's act of self-immolation became the catalyst for the Tunisian Revolution and the wider Arab Spring.[34] Within hours of his funeral, a nationwide protest was ignited, which led to the resignation of Tunisian dictator Zine El Abidine Ben Ali.

The tragic story of a fruit vendor became the heroic story of a nation that rose in unison against an oppressive regime. Did this event surge overnight, or was it the outcome of years of wrongful policies by the Tunisian government?

In most countries, government is the leading cause of injustice and oppression. Men and women with wrongful ideologies come into power either through an election, appointment, revolution, inheritance, manipulation, or corruption and commit crimes against the people they should be serving. Spiritual Activists have a duty to stand up against oppressive regimes, for they wield their power wrongfully and disproportionately. Sadly, most people don't realize a wrongful act has been committed until years later. They stand up to protest, but in reality somebody should have raised a fist much earlier.

The naïve observer is unable to connect the dots and thinks that Bouazizi committed self-immolation because he was unable to sell fruit. When in reality, Bouazizi's fate was sealed when Ben Ali chose to become a dictator twenty-four years earlier and set the country in a direction that would have dire consequences.

The naïve observer only sees the very last straw that breaks the camel's back, without realizing that the pains of wrongful policies are felt and seen long after they are voted on the legislative floor. The naïve observer believes that the recent actions of an elected politician are to blame for the pains they feel today. The truth is that the real culprit is the collective set of laws that over time build on each other to create the current conditions. Like heated water slowly reaching a boiling point, oppressive and abusive trends are the real forces behind oppressive laws. It is the duty of every Spiritual Activist to diligently observe rising political trends, unmask their hidden agendas and warn the people of the wrongful directions they face. It is the duty of the Spiritual Activist to paint the larger picture, so citizens can know how their vote will influence the future. For ultimately, oppressive trends reach a boiling point only after years of applying heat.

The Arab Spring was an inevitable outcome of extreme inequality reaching a boiling point. It was the inevitable outcome of political and economic decisions made solely to provide for the elite class. The naïve observer may think that this was a problem only of Arab dictatorships, and may not realize this is a reality that resides close to home. The Arab Spring is similar to the Occupy Wall Street movement, and the people of Tunisia are not much different from the people in the United States and other Western nations. If we were to put aside the obvious differences of government, religion, language, and culture, we would find some significant similarities between these nations and the ruling elites that govern them. If we were to look for a common factor that contributes to the oppression of any people, we would find systemic conditions created by government policies: the erasing of lines that separate the public and private sectors squeezing the resources of hard working citizens. These are not isolated events. They are part of larger, oppressive trends.

Only a few years before Bouazizi doused himself with gasoline the conditions for a similar boiling point were being set across the United States. Rebecca, like many other citizens, felt fortunate. For ten years she held a good job at a large firm that specializes in financial and insurance services. In February 2008, at age forty-four, she was laid off along with the top tier of the company. She diligently applied for job openings every week, but the recklessness of Wall Street and the fall of AIG made the financial and insurance environment hostile to new employment. So, she began to apply for other positions only to find she was one applicant among hundreds. Rebecca continued her search of job openings that were worthy of her experience and education, but found that most companies were not hiring. She was forced to apply for jobs in the service sector, but she was repeatedly turned down for being overqualified. After one year of being unemployed, Rebecca exhausted her unemployment benefits, her "rainy-day fund," and her retirement savings. Her home state of California has restrictions on benefits, which forced her to hit rock bottom before additional monies were distributed. In the meantime, her two children depended on her ability to provide. With every month that passed, her chances of finding employment diminished. After submitting more than two thousand resumes, Rebecca was forced into poverty. It is an ironic and tragic narrative: a family living among the upper class, losing everything to the forces of greed and forced to live below the poverty line. In the fall of 2010, Rebecca and her children moved into low-income housing. Needless to say, she was terrified.[35]

How different is Rebecca from Bouazizi? How different is an unemployed manager in California from an unemployed fruit vendor in Tunisia? Putting aside cultural, language, ethnic, and religious differences, what do they have in common? After all, pain is pain. How many years of unemployment could she stomach before reaching her boiling point? Most likely, Rebecca will not douse herself with gasoline and set herself on fire, but she is kneeling before a government structure and asking the same question: "How do you expect me to make a living?"

Rebecca and others are desperately hoping to be heard. What is not certain is if the House of Representatives is listening. How do people living in democratic countries fight for change? Short of setting ourselves on fire, what do we have to do in order to be heard? Fortunately, in the United States and other democratic countries there are political mechanisms in place that allow for Rebecca's voice to be heard. There are many elected politicians who are honestly trying to pass laws that would help Americans get back to work. Yet there are others whose language reveals a bias, portraying the unemployed people as lazy.

Republican presidential hopeful Newt Gingrich gave the following description of poor people while campaigning in Des Moines, Iowa for the 2012 elections:

"Really poor children in really poor neighborhoods have no habits of working and have nobody around them who works . . . so they literally have no habit of showing up on Monday. They have no habit of staying all day. They have no habit of 'I do this and you give me cash,' unless it's illegal." [36]

Such broad-sweeping, negative descriptions of people living in poverty demonstrate Mr. Gingrich's bias and inability to connect with people from lower economic classes. How would Rebecca's children feel about this statement? Months later, while campaigning for the same presidential election, Governor Mitt Romney spoke derisively about the working poor. "I'll never convince them they should take personal responsibility and care for their lives."[37] This comment illustrates an economic class bias that keeps wealthy people, like Governor Romney, from understanding the plight of the working poor. How can two candidates have such compatible negative views? Is it just a coincidence or is it a problem created by the enormous economic divide between the ultra-rich and the working poor? These are not isolated events. They are part of a larger, oppressive trend. Knowing that other politicians suffer from the same bias, it is imperative that Spiritual Activists advocate for the poor, for they may not be able to speak on their own behalf when legislation is being debated. Unfortunately, too many spiritual people shy away from becoming activists because they loathe the political arena.

The hard truth is that a Spiritual Activist has no option but to be political. For it's not about being a Democrat or a Republican. It's not about getting pulled into the culture wars. It is about the same issue the prophet Micah preached 2730 years ago: justice.

The God of Jesus and of Moses, the God of Sarah and of the Virgin Mary is a God of justice. To be a Spiritual Activist is to be concerned with justice; because Rebecca's job could have been saved years earlier; thirty years earlier, to be exact, when former President Ronald Reagan was promoting a trickle down economy. A Spiritual Activist would have identified Reagan's trickle down economic policies as unjust and unethical. Likewise, a Spiritual Activist would have denounced former President Clinton's repeal of the Glass-Steagall Act as unjust, for it transformed the banking and financial culture allowing the big players to always come out winning and the small consumers to be squeezed a bit tighter. Both administrations, Reagan's and Clinton's, were caught up in the exuberant energy of an egocentric financial culture that in the short term generated revenues, but in the long term made upward mobility very difficult for the lower and middle class workers of the nation. These are not isolated events. They are part of a larger oppressive trend that can only be changed through political action.

Consequently, Spiritual Activists need to seek economic justice by looking at the bigger picture and condemning policies that at their core promote inequality. It could be argued that Rebecca should have found employment in one of the many service industries available. These are jobs in the food service, housekeeping or retail industry. However, finding employment in the service sectors does not necessarily pull her out of poverty. In the last thirty years, service sector jobs have not kept up with the rising cost of living.[38] It used to be that people working in the service sector could afford the life style of middle class Americans.

Today, they are known as poverty jobs with wages so low that they force a person to work over seventy hours a week. Is it fair for people to make less than a living wage in any sector of the job market? A survey taken by the Public Religion Research Institute[39] found that over two-thirds of Americans favor raising the minimum to $10 an hour. Why? Because the population recognizes what the corporate sector refuses to admit: better wages will create a better economy for the whole nation.

Economic justice is not only concerned with finding Rebecca a job. Economic justice is also concerned with changing the systemic problems that keep whole communities trapped in endless cycles of poverty. Economic justice is creating fair and balanced conditions that will prevent future economic disasters that somehow still benefit the end-of-year bonuses of Wall Street brokers while devastating the working poor. Like it or not, economic justice requires entering the political arena.

March 25, 2011, was the one hundred-year anniversary of the Triangle Shirtwaist Company fire that claimed the lives of 146 laborers, two of whom were only fourteen years old. The tragic fire helped spawn a labor reform movement that eventually led to the formation of thirty-six labor laws in the state of New York. The movement continued, forming the National Labor Relations Act (also known as the Wagner Act) passed in 1935, which gave workers the right to form unions and to collectively bargain with their employers. The twenty-four-year journey to enact such important legislation took persistence and the work of many activists. It was legislation of this sort that allowed our ancestors to work in healthy environments and receive benefits that promoted a higher quality of life. Yet such noble legislation took twenty-four years to enact.

If there is one reality that has become increasingly evident, it is the growing difficulty for the US government to enact laws that benefit the people. Even high school students studying American history can see with their innocent eyes how inefficient our government is becoming. Why has our political process become fundamentally flawed to the point that it seeks to protect the rights of businesses over the rights of individuals? Why have the needs of the "free market" superseded the needs of the people? These questions deserve an entire bookcase of expert analysis in order to properly develop them. Yet we must not be intimidated by the overwhelming complexities of the political process. We must seek to understand the different knots that bind up good legislation in order to effectively create change. Consequently, Spiritual Activists must, at the very least, become familiar with the political process; for it is there that lasting change can be enacted.

The political process is like a chain in which every link is important to its health. This chain connects the healthy values of the people to the laws that govern their community. If one link on the chain is weakened, the entire process is weakened. This interdependence requires that each link be present and strong. The chain is usually strongest at the level of local government, where the direct correlation between the people and the policies can be traced. The chain is usually weakest, and ultimately broken into different segments, at the federal level where the voice of the people struggles to make its way to the legislative floor.

At one end of this chain we have government. Government is most often directed through the legislative process. The legislative process is directed through advocacy. Advocacy is directed through organized groups, which in turn are directed by value systems. Value systems are directed by the community, which is directed by the voices of its residents. The importance of the Spiritual Activist in this chain is evident at every level to protect the voice of the people along the way. The three branches of the U.S. government allow for the Spiritual Activist to advocate in different settings should the legislative process become corrupt.

Since 1981, the country has witnessed the priority of the political process shift from people to corporations. Whereas once it was the needs of the people that elicited legislation, it now is increasingly the needs of corporations. Without a doubt, the rights and voice of the people have become secondary to those of the corporate sector. Let me be clear, the problem is not the insertion of corporations into the political process. After all, the business community of the nation deserves to be protected under the law. The problem lies with an ideology that ascribes the "free market" as virtuous, giving it priority over the rights of people for basic services.[40] It is an ideology of "trickle-down economics" that since 1981 has created a capitalistic focus that benefits the top quintile of the nation and in 2010 declared multinational corporations equal to people. This ideology has been promoted by Wrongful Activists and enacted into policy at both the state and federal levels. Consequently, a tug-of-war between ideologies is tearing the chain apart and grinding the wheels of the legislative progress to a standstill. Time and time again we witness the blatant catering of politicians to the business and finance sector at the expense of the people's welfare. These are politicians whose legislative priority is clearly business over people, capitalism over humanity, and profit over a clean environment. These politicians are to be identified and categorized as wrongful politicians. The rise of wrongful politicians is connected to the rise of Wrongful Activists, for they emerge from the same environment that promotes wrongful ideas. Wrongful politicians no longer serve the people, for they are the indentured servants of the corporate and finance sector. They neglect the long-term benefits of the people for the short-term benefits of corporate earnings.

To be fair, wrongful politicians have existed since the beginning of organized politics. They were among us in the beginning of the nineteenth century as the Union was being torn apart by a separatist movement that led to the Civil War. We saw them take office during the McCarthy era and the Red Scare. We have witnessed wrongful politicians enact laws that plunder the earth and its resources for the sake of corporate profits. The recent rise of wrongful politicians is alarming. Spiritual Activists must carefully examine elected public officials and watch for the signs of wrongful behavior, for inevitably these officials will seek to further the interests of corporations over the interests of the people.

The wrongful politician will try to block legislative efforts designed to improve the quality of life for individuals and communities. For example, the Lilly Ledbetter Fair Pay Act, ensuring that women get equal pay for equal work, met innumerable obstacles during its ten year struggle to be signed. As common sense as this concept of equality may be, the Lilly Ledbetter Fair Pay Act was repeatedly opposed during the Bush presidency. President Obama signed it into law within days of being sworn into office. The Affordable Care Act, also known as Obama Care, at its core is driven by the welfare of the citizenry, not the insurance companies or the corporate sector. Yet, wrongful politicians want to repeal it, stating that it is not in the best interest of the country for every citizen to have Universal Health Care. Clearly, this is a wrongful stance that advocates for the profit earnings of strong corporations over the rights of the weak.

Despite the recent efforts of politicians with a humanitarian focus, other legislative efforts have been passed that benefit solely the business and financial sectors. Consider that during the nation's worst epidemic of obesity and nutrition-related illnesses, Congress brought a bill to the floor on November 17, 2011, that would facilitate a lunch program that provides pizza and French fries in public schools receiving subsidies. It passed seven days later as part of a larger spending bill. With the many urgent and critical needs of the nation, the US House of Representatives decided to slip a few lines redefining tomato paste as a vegetable serving. Why? Who benefits when such language is enacted into laws? To answer that question, one only needs to see who is celebrating the passing of the bill.

"It's an important victory," said Corey Henry, spokesman for the American Frozen Food Institute. The AFI had lobbied Congress on behalf of frozen pizza sellers like ConAgra Foods Inc. and Schwan Food Co. and French fries makers McCain Foods Ltd. and J. R. Simplot Co.; the latter is best known as a supplier to fast food company McDonald's Corp.[41] Supporters of this bill may counter with the following question: "If parents don't want their child to eat pizza, shouldn't they pack them a lunch?" The response is simple. It is wrongful to place the interest of corporate earnings over the interest of children living in poverty whose parents don't have the resources to prepare a healthy lunch.

For Spiritual Activists, it is important to use the political process to enact change and stop wrongful legislation from being passed. Sometimes a justice effort can find an elected official to champion a cause. More often than not, justice efforts must find a way, even if it is called political coercion, to move politicians to vote in a rightful manner. Changing a politician's point of view is not easy. It is here where political strategy and fieldwork are needed to convince the politician of the rightful vote. Political strategies usually involve any of the following tactics:

1. Voter registration drives
2. Petition drives
3. Community forums
4. Endorsements from the faith community
5. Endorsements from the business sector and the chamber of commerce
6. Attendance at local town hall meetings in significant numbers
7. Visits to the local office of the elected official
8. Letters or phone calls to the elected official
9. Meetings and dialogues with the elected official
10. Voting on Election Day

Rising Political Trends

In the field of political activism, it is important to anticipate rising trends that influence the political scene. Al-Qaeda's attack on September 11, 2001, traumatized our nation. Only in hindsight can we look at ourselves, examine the wounds that were created by such an attack, and realize that many of the policies and rhetoric that followed were a natural consequences of that attack. Unfortunately, a snowball effect was created that demonized Muslims, scapegoated immigrants, and justified torture. To question the policies of the government was to be unpatriotic. To allow for different points of view was perceived as being sympathetic with the "enemies of the nation." Clearly, a new tide was rising in the political and cultural climate after September 11, 2001, and it was sweeping everyone. It was difficult to be a Spiritual Activist in those days, for the new political current was strong, and few were able to swim against it.

A Spiritual Activist should not allow herself to be carried away by the political currents that ebb and flow. A Spiritual Activist must keep her objectivity and identify wrongful behavior when it emerges. To keep silent does not help. How many people were afraid to speak against Adolf Hitler and regretted it later? How many people were swept by the rising tide of fascism and became part of a genocide that the world will always condemn?

It could be argued that the change in the US political climate is nowhere near the political climate of Nazi Germany in 1936. That argument is valid. Yet it could also be argued that there are plenty of reasons to be concerned. History has proven that fascism emerges from communities that are economically depressed and need a release valve to vent frustrations. Fascism emerges as a natural reaction to protect resources from the people considered to be different. Has the nation's Great Recession created a climate for fascist ideologies to rise once again? To help us answer this question, we need to look at the characteristics of fascism. Dr. Lawrence Britt, a political scientist, has examined the fascist regimes of Hitler (Germany); Mussolini (Italy); Franco (Spain); Suharto (Indonesia); Papadopoulos (Greece); Salazar (Portugal); and Pinochet (Chile). Britt found fourteen defining characteristics[42] common to each:

1. **Powerful and Continuing Nationalism.** Fascist regimes tend to make constant use of patriotic mottos, slogans, symbols, songs, and other paraphernalia. Flags are seen everywhere, as are flag symbols on clothing and in public displays.

2. **Disdain for the Recognition of Human Rights.** Out of fear of enemies and the need for security, the people in fascist regimes are persuaded that human rights can be ignored in certain cases because of "need."

3. **Identification of Enemies/Scapegoats as a Unifying Cause.** The people are rallied into a unifying patriotic frenzy over the need to eliminate a perceived threat: racial, ethnic, or religious minorities; liberals; communists; socialists; terrorists; etc.

4. **Supremacy of the Military.** Even when there are widespread domestic problems, the military is given a disproportionate amount of government funding, and the

domestic agenda is neglected. Soldiers and military service are glamorized.

5. **Rampant Sexism.** The governments of fascist nations tend to be almost exclusively male-dominated. Under fascist regimes, traditional gender roles are made more rigid. Divorce, abortion, and homosexuality are suppressed and the state is represented as the ultimate guardian of the family institution.

6. **Controlled Mass Media.** Sometimes the media is directly controlled by the government, but in other cases the media is indirectly controlled by government regulation, or sympathetic media spokespeople and executives. Censorship, especially in wartime, is very common.

7. **Obsession with National Security.** Fear is used as a motivational tool by the government over the masses.

8. **Religion and Government Are Intertwined.** Governments in fascist nations tend to use the most common religion in the nation as a tool to manipulate public opinion. Religious rhetoric and terminology are common from government leaders, even when the major tenets of the religion are diametrically opposed to the government's policies or actions.

9. **Corporate Power Is Protected.** The industrial and business aristocracy of a fascist nation often are the ones who put the government leaders into power, creating a mutually beneficial business/government relationship and power elite.

10. **Labor Power Is Suppressed**. The organizing power of labor is a real threat to a fascist government. Labor unions are either eliminated or are severely suppressed.

11. **Disdain for Intellectuals and the Arts.** Fascist nations tend to promote open hostility to academia. It is not uncommon for professors and other academics to be censored or even arrested. Free expression in the arts and letters is openly attacked.

12. **Obsession with Crime and Punishment.** Under fascist regimes, the police are given almost limitless power to enforce laws. The people are often willing to overlook police abuses and even forgo civil liberties in the name of patriotism. There is often a national police force with virtually unlimited power in fascist nations.

13. **Rampant Cronyism and Corruption.** Fascist regimes almost always are governed by groups of friends and associates who appoint each other to government positions and use governmental power and authority to protect their friends from accountability.

14. **Fraudulent Elections.** Sometimes elections in fascist nations are a complete sham. Other times elections are manipulated by smear campaigns against or even assassination of opposition candidates, use of legislation to control voting numbers or political district boundaries, and manipulation of the media. Fascist nations also typically use their judiciaries to manipulate or control elections.

Recognizing that in politics, as well as in religion, the flow from the conservative right to the liberal left is often just a matter of degrees, it is an interesting exercise to see how many of Dr. Britt's identifying marks of fascism are showing themselves in the United States. Most likely, the United States will never go the route of Nazi Germany or Franco's Spain because of the sheer size of the nation, the diversity of the citizenry, and the many news organizations that keep a close eye on the political process. However, it is possible for smaller pockets of the nation, states, or municipalities to be ruled by politicians who hold such extreme conservative views. It is a tangible, historical fact that certain municipalities of the nation held a collective ideology that was dangerously close to fascism. Prior to the civil rights movement, several Southern states contained pockets of fascism that had managed to imbed itself deeply into the political and judicial structures of government.

Consider the assassination of NAACP leader Medgar Evers in Mississippi the evening of June 12, 1963. Only a highly structured system designed to promote injustice could acquit Byron de la Beckwith from that crime. That Evers was the victim of a hate crime is tragic, but what is deplorable is that the judicial system of the day did not recognize Evers death as a crime. Fascism was alive and well during those dark years, and unfortunately we can still find remnants of it. The Southern Poverty Law Center reports that fascist ideologies are readily recognizable in the many white supremacist organizations that abide throughout the nation and manage to influence local governments.[43]

Spiritual Activists have to be aware of dangerous political trends and help people realize the direction that such ultraconservative agendas can lead to. It is clear that in 2010 a new wave of conservative voices emerged on the political scene. How conservative are these new voices? Some would argue that they are dangerously close to fascism. Presidential hopeful, Rick Santorum fueled the wave of anti-intellectualism that emerged from the Tea Party rhetoric by calling universities "indoctrination mills."[44] For a presidential candidate to openly state such negative views illustrates how anti-intellectualism is growing among conservatives. The disdain for higher education was also heard in the rhetoric of conservative pundit, Rush Limbaugh,[45] who openly spoke disparagingly of people with graduate degrees. Sadly, Limbaugh and Santorum's opinion is also shared by policy makers for it has led to unfriendly education policies in states with a Republican leadership, specifically in Wisconsin, Texas and Florida.

In Texas, the Republican Party 2012 political platform openly declared its opposition to the teaching of higher order thinking skills and critical thinking skills in the public schools.[46] This platform begs the question: what kind of future will Texas have if children never learn how to think critically? In Wisconsin, Governor Scott Walker successfully managed to convince state legislators that their public school teachers no longer had a right to be organized. This issue caused weeks of protest in Wisconsin and led over a million voters to campaign against Governor Walker. If budgets are a statement of our beliefs, then Florida Governor, Rick Scott, demonstrated in 2011 where his bias lies. In the spring of 2011 Governor Scott presented a budget that "eviscerated the K-12 public school programs and shifted those earnings to the private sector."[47] Convinced by Santorum that colleges are the breeding ground for liberals, Governor Scott re-appointed mayor campaign contributor, Carlos Beruff, [48] to the State College of Florida (SCF) Board of Trustees to carry out his ultra-conservative agenda. Beruff, elected Board Chair by six other Scott appointees, began an immediate attack on traditional academic operations and orchestrated a plan to remove Dr. Lars Hafner from the SCF presidency. [49] Hafner, a former Democratic state representative and strong proponent of the liberal arts as the cornerstone of critical thinking, had been praised by his former Board for transforming the college into a four-year institution and establishing innovative programs.[50] Dr. Hafner's experience with Governor Scott is more than an isolated event. It is part of a larger, anti-intellectual and oppressive trend. Texas, Wisconsin and Florida are only the most glaring examples of the anti-intellectualism wave reaching legislative levels. Other states around the nation have heard similar rhetoric from their elected leaders. It is only natural to ask, "What is going on?" Could it be argued that this is one of Dr. Britt's signs of rising fascism?

As of the fall of 2012, it is not clear if the American voters have fully understood how an ultra-conservative political agenda will affect public education. It is not clear if the American voters understand that the nation's problems are the consequences of economic policies that for the last thirty years were aimed at benefiting the corporate and finance sector. It is not clear if the average voter understands that the economic policies that led this country to experience the Great Recession and the largest economic gap between rich and poor could easily be restored by a conservative administration. What is clear is that the work of the Spiritual Activist is more important than ever. The work of every Spiritual Activist has to reach the political arena, for it is there where the most important battles are being fought. If spiritual people in America don't become active in promoting systemic change then the fate of Tunisia is not too far from our own reality. Let us work together so that no other person suffers the same fate as that of a Tunisian fruit vendor.

CONCLUSION

Human Nature and the Need for Spiritual Activists

A scorpion befriended a ladybug, who became a loyal companion to him. A time came when she struggled to cross a challenging and dangerous river, and so the scorpion offered to take her to the other side on his back. He had come to care for her and promised he would never harm her. But, safely across the river, he allowed his tail to dip upon her with its venomous sting. As she lay in greatest pain, she said, "But, you promised . . . why?" He shrugged and said sadly, "Because it is my nature."

~Aesop

The essence of human nature has been debated for centuries around the world. Aristotle, Francis Bacon, Thomas Aquinas, Thomas Hobbes, and many other philosophers presented their argument on the nature of humanity in order to explain good and evil in our world. Postmodern philosophy, as well as popular culture today, declares humans as inherently good. Yet it was not too long ago when the dominant view was that people were inherently evil, born with Original Sin. This view led the Puritans to believe the "evil" in their children was to be removed through proper parenting, which often included beatings. "Spare the rod and spoil the child" was one of their maxims. For progressive people, the word "evil" becomes a distraction from the true issue. People who focus on evil may find themselves blaming their problems on "the Devil," an anthropomorphic effort to counter the human qualities ascribed to God.

Mencius, a Confucian philosopher (372-289 BCE), argued that human nature was inherently good, and in defense of that argument he wrote the following: "All men have a mind which cannot bear to see the suffering of others. For example, if you suddenly see a child about to fall into a well, your first reaction is to save her. You don't do this for the sake of befriending the child's parent or to gain praise from the public; you do it out of your original good nature . . . . The way man loses his original good nature is like the trees in a mountain that are being subjected to endless disturbances . . . . If a man is constantly subjected to disturbances, negative influence, his character is bound to be affected accordingly, despite occasional good education. But that is not his original nature. His original nature is good. The evil in him is a result of external influence." [51]

Twenty-three hundred years have passed since Mencius offered this analogy, and it definitely speaks to the debate between nature and nurture. The "child in the well" analogy has been used often to describe the inherently good nature of human beings. But how do we explain the individual who would walk away from a child in the well or the individual who would push a child into a well? We can't. Such an act has no explanation. We stand in horror knowing there are people capable of such acts.

This analogy goes beyond the personal sense of ethics. It can be an analogy for the decisions governments or large corporations make to save other communities that are "trapped in a well" of violence and despair. Unfortunately, many corporations and governments fail the compassion test, and over the years we have witnessed the bullying of much weaker and vulnerable communities until they fall into a well of economic hardship. Often these decisions are justified as standard business practice in order to increase profit margins or to protect American interests abroad.

A good example of this failed compassion is how the pharmaceutical companies structure their prices for lifesaving drugs. Throughout the 1990s Sub-Saharan Africa had an AIDS crisis of biblical proportions. More people were dying in South Africa of AIDS than of all other causes combined. The pharmaceutical company Bristol-Myers Squibb (BMS) set a price for each tablet of antiretroviral drug at about $4.50. The dosage was two tablets a day. In a developed nation, this sounds like a reasonable price for a lifesaving medication. For people living in abject poverty, it is beyond their reach. The average person living in the slums of South Africa would be unable to pay the $9 per day, or $270 per month. Knowing the global scope of AIDS and the need for a treatment, BMS was able to secure a patent in every continent, giving it the sole right to produce, distribute, and set pricing for the medication worldwide.[52] When BMS refused to lower its prices, the government of South Africa began to produce generic versions of the drug and distribute it to its residents for free.

In March 1999, with the help of Vice President Al Gore, BMS made an effort to take the government of South Africa to court for the purpose of stopping it from manufacturing a generic version of the drug.[53] Many activists stepped forward to advocate on behalf of the South African people, but the solution was layered behind complicated economic terms and procedures.

Stop. Did you catch that? Three sentences back . . . Vice President Al Gore was assisting a pharmaceutical company with a lawsuit. How many dots can we connect with this statement? Why is the second-most powerful man in the world, who was a presidential candidate for the 2000 elections, doing the dirty work for a pharmaceutical company? What does that say about the relationship between government and multinational companies, between politicians and corporate interests? With such a heavy hitter on the side of BMS, South Africa had to call upon the world community in order to stand a fighting chance. The world community came to South Africa's aid. Thousands upon thousands of activists, most notably Archbishop Desmond Tutu, Dr. Paul Farmer, James Love, Ralph Nader, and many others showed their support in one form or another.

After a long legal battle, BMS agreed to a concession, making it possible for the South African population to purchase antiretroviral drugs at affordable prices. The South African people were now able to receive treatment. However, this didn't magically happen overnight, and several years passed before the antiretroviral drugs were able to reach the people.

Unfortunately, the AIDS epidemic had spiraled out of control by 2000, and it took an unprecedented effort to reverse the mortality rate. The Actuarial Society of South Africa estimated that from 2002 to 2008 an average 704 people per day were dying in South Africa from AIDS-related illnesses, or 257,000 per year.[54] By 2010, after a multi-agency effort the annual mortality rate dropped to 190,000. More than 67,000 people lived to see another year thanks to the wider accessibility of antiretroviral drugs. This is more than a number. We are talking about 67,000 people who were able to provide for their children, smile, hug, and love.

It is probably fair to say that most of the business and government leaders who were withholding the antiretroviral drugs from the South African government would jump into a well to save a trapped child. Mencius would claim their human nature as good. But what is it about the business sector that would take humanity's compassion and label it as a bad business decision? More importantly, why does the rest of society tolerate it? We all know men and women who would risk their lives without hesitation to save a child. Yet those same people vote for political agendas that keep corporations from facing regulations, many of which protect the earth and save human lives.

The study of human nature is concerned with the question of why people make wrongful and harmful decisions. If we were to adopt Mencius's view, that every person is inherently good, then the question needs to be modified. Why do people, who are inherently good, surrender their ethical framework when they are part of a larger system? This was true of the many Germans who yielded their sense of right and wrong to the larger Nazi movement. Although it is an extreme example it is relevant, for the same forces are at work when people of faith put aside their spiritual/religious values for the sake of corporate earnings. Consequently, the question is no longer about human nature but about the forces that influence human nature. Mencius argued that *the evil in humankind is a result of external influence.* In our twenty-first-century world, the external influence that pushes humans to make wrongful business decisions is the finance and corporate sector. Therefore, Spiritual Activists must also look at the broader system that breeds such wrongful behavior.

In 2009, Bernard (Bernie) Lawrence Madoff was arrested for fraud for having the longest-running and largest Ponzi scheme in the history of the stock market. Madoff managed to run a fraudulent investment scheme for more than twenty-five years, earning in excess of sixty-five billion dollars. Thousands of people lost their life savings. Bernie Madoff was sentenced to one hundred fifty years in prison. When Madoff's wife was interviewed, she stated she considered her husband a good man who would never intentionally hurt anyone. Is it fair to say she believes her husband would save a child from falling in a well? Probably. The Madoff scandal brings to light several questions. Why would a person who would jump into a well to save a child commit such fraud on Wall Street? Was Madoff encouraged by a society that rewards the accumulation of wealth at the expense of others? How much of the Madoff scandal is the sin of one man and how much is the sin of the system?

Spiritual activism is forced to look at systems and demand change so systemic wrongs can be stopped from occurring again. Spiritual activism needs to instill basic human and faith values like compassion and fairness into the larger systems. The work of a Spiritual Activist is to remind people that our faith and value system is not to be tucked away when we go to the office. The work of a Spiritual Activist is to constantly remind people that how we treat our neighbor, client, business competitor, or enemy is to be in accordance with our faith.

Unfortunately, human nature allows for wrongful thought and behavior to be embraced and institutionalized. It is the work of Spiritual Activists to persevere until those wrongs are repaired. In the Jewish faith there is a term, *tikkun olam*, which means "to repair the world." Tikkun olam is more than just a theological phrase; it is a duty. Likewise, the Spiritual Activist, regardless of religious background, feels a duty to repair the world.

The world is going through many changes. Many new technological advances offer promising hope for a better tomorrow. Yet they also bring new dangers. Theologian Gustavo Gutierrez argues in his treatise for liberation theology that the poor of the world will continue to experience oppression because of the technological advances that only widen the gap between the economic classes.[55] The next generation of Spiritual Activists must be prepared to fight a large system that has institutionalized wrongful policies behind layers of complicated economic terms. Systems that breed the Bernie Madoffs of the world must be forced to change. Multinational companies that manipulate elected leaders must be forced to stop. The question is how?

Get Angry . . . Get Very Angry

A righteous wrath propels people into action. There is an empowerment that surges forward when we tap into the anger deep within us. This anger moved thousands of people to protest the unfair policies that kept South Africans from accessing antiretroviral drugs. This anger swept across the nation and created the Occupy Wall Street movement. Only people who become angry, instead of indifferent, can stand up and protest the wrongful policies that have created harm to so many people. It does not take a professor to recognize that something is very wrong with the various systems of our world. We may not know what to do about it, but to stand up and name the wrong is a first step.

People are needed to stand up for the rights of the "children who are thrown down a well," be they the homeless, immigrant, hungry, or destitute. But first we must shake the indifference that afflicts our land. We must desensitize the many people watching as if it were an HBO special and stir in them the righteous wrath. Move them into action and shake them from complacency. Reach for their innermost sense of what God's purpose is for humanity on Earth, and they will respond. Most people lack an in-depth knowledge of theology, the Bible, or doctrines, but they do have an innate sense of what is a wrongful intention for God's creation. Let them know that God is on the side of justice. Empower them to stand up, for God's sake, and make a difference. Let them get angry—very angry—and lead them to correct what is wrong. Become the leader, the Spiritual Activist God is calling you to be. Use the principles and strategies given to you in this book, and others, to create systemic change that will benefit the world.

You Are Divinely Called

Know you are loved by God and are called by God to bring justice, fairness, and joy to those who have suffered oppression. The Spirit of God will help us with this difficult task by providing for us the inner resources we need. God has always relied on men and women to bring about the shift of consciousness and to untie the shackles of oppression that keep us from enjoying all of Creation. Change will not come by itself.

At times, in my pastorate, I hear people express a spiritual immaturity for God to solve their problems. Like the child whose doting parent does the science fair project for him, there are people who expect for God to do our work. When we pray for wisdom, God does not magically give us extra IQ points. Instead, we might find ourselves in a situation from which we emerge wiser. Likewise, when we pray for an injustice to end or a situation to change, God will not magically interfere. Instead, we might find ourselves with the right opportunity to exercise our choice to stand up and be counted.

Do not think of God as the magical provider of all we need. Instead, consider God our partner who works and suffers by our side to overcome injustice. Let go of your doubt and wholly embrace the Spirit of God. Let go of your cynicism and dip your soul into the Spirit of God. It is a wellspring of strength, patience, and insight. Release your fears and know you are divinely called to be a Spiritual Activist. Stand up against the Wrongful Activist and know God is speaking through your voice. March to the protest site and know God is moving through your steps. Feed your brothers and sisters with hope for a better day and know your hands are God's hands.

God is calling us—tikkun olam—to repair the world. God is calling us to help create a new world, one that will not measure individuals by their purchasing power or net worth. God is calling each and every one of us to stand up and raise our voices in unison against the powers that rape the earth, pollute our children, enslave our women, and rob us of joy. Let us answer God's call. Answer the call and you will find the joy of bringing a smile to another's face. Answer the call and you will find the strength of standing in unison. Answer the call and your life will become vibrant, aware of all that is good around you. Laughter and joy will bubble forth with ease, bringing hope to those around you. And love will become the healthiest expression of God's relationship with you.

Love is the natural outcome of a life with God. Choose God, and you will love generously, without bounds. You will love deeply and passionately, stirring in others the same desire for love. Your love will transcend all that is superficial and vain. And after living the love that flows from living with God, you will know what it means to love your neighbor; to love your enemy; to love yourself. Through this love you will know how to forgive and be forgiven. Through this love you will forgive the Wrongful Activists for they know not what they do. Through this love you will be able to appreciate all life has to offer, all the human touch can be, and all the joy there is in even the smallest of gestures.

God is calling us because God wants us to love. Answer the call. A life of love beyond measure awaits you. Answer the call. A life of spiritual activism awaits you. God is calling you. Answer God's call.

ABOUT THE AUTHOR

The Reverend Dr. Guillermo Márquez-Sterling is the youngest son of Cuban exiled parents. Although born in Miami, Florida he was raised in Puerto Rico. He has multiple academic degrees and has lived a life of service, first as a public school teacher and currently as a Christian pastor. His passion is to help people help themselves and to promote a healthy and progressive image of God that is inclusive and empowering. He lives in Miami with his beautiful wife and family.

Guillermo Márquez-Sterling being handcuffed at a sit-down protest for fair labor conditions at the University of Miami (March, 2006)

BIBLIOGRAPHY
AND SUGGESTED READING

Allison, Michael and Jude Kaye. *Strategic Planning for Nonprofit Organizations: A Practical Guide and Workbook*. Hoboken, NJ: Wiley, 2003.

Borg, Marcus. *Speaking Christian*. New York: Harper One, 2011.

Carter, Jimmy. *Palestine: Peace, Not Apartheid*. New York: Simon & Schuster, 2007.

Chang, Ha-Joon. *23 Things They Don't Tell You about Capitalism*. New York: Bloomsbury Press, 2011.

Chomsky, Noam. *Profit over People: Neoliberalism and Global Order*. New York: Seven Stories Press, 1999.

Dalai Lama, HH. *The Art of Happiness: A Handbook for Living*. New York: Riverhead Books, 1998.

Foster, Richard J. *Celebration of Discipline: The Path to Spiritual Growth*. San Francisco: Harper Collins Publishers, 1988.

Gutierrez, Gustavo. *A Theology of Liberation*. Maryknoll, NY: Orbis Books, 1971

King Jr., Martin Luther. *Strength to Love*. Minneapolis: Fortress Press, 1963.

Rohr, Richard. *Simplicity*. New York: Crossroads Publishing, 1990.

Skocpol, Theda and Vanessa Williamson. *The Tea Party and the Remaking of Republican Conservatism.* Oxford: University Press, 2012.

Smith, Huston. *The World's Religions.* San Francisco: Harper Collins, 1991.

Tolstoy, Leo. *Spiritual Writings.* Maryknoll, NY: Orbis Books, 2006

Wink, Walter. *Engaging the Powers.* Minneapolis: Fortress Press, 1992.

Additional Sources and Suggested Reading

Borg, Marcus. *The Heart of Christianity: Rediscovering a Life of Faith.*

Heschel, Abraham Joshua. *God in Search of Man.*

Lerner, Michael. *The Left Hand of God.*

Meeks, M. Douglas. *God the Economist.*

Morewedge, Parviz. *Islamic Philosophical Theology.*

ENDNOTES

1   Noam Chomsky. "The Responsibility of Intellectuals," *New York Review of Books*. 1967.

2   Marcus Borg. *Speaking Christian*.

3   Teachings from the Dalai Lama, www.dalailama.com/teachings/training-the-mind/verse-2

4   Anderson, Bernhard. *Understanding the Old Testament*. Prentice Hall: New Jersey, 1986, 50.

5   Exodus 2:15-4:17

6   Farid Mirbagheri. *Islam and Liberal Peace*; www.st-andrews.ac.uk/intrel/media/Mirbagheri_Islam_and_liberal_peace.pdf

7   Feminist Wire; November 1999. AFLM was founded by Andrew Burnett, who in 1993 began a signature campaign promoting "justifiable homicide" against doctors and staff of clinics that perform abortions. Burnett published and distributed the book *A Time to Kill* by Michael Bray, who is a convicted bomber of abortion clinics. The AFLM closed in 1999 due to lack of support and after losing a civil lawsuit by Planned Parenthood.

8   Martin Luther King Jr. May 1966.

9   Martin Luther King Jr. *Stride toward Freedom: The Montgomery Story*. Beacon Press, 1958.

10 Jimmy Carter. *Palestine: Peace, Not Apartheid*.

11 The Kairos Document

12   Noam Chomsky. *Profit over People: Neoliberalism and Global Order*. Seven Story Press, 1999.

13   Huffington Post; October 6, 2011.

14   http://usgovinfo.about.com/od/thepresidentandcabinet/a/did-bush-say-go-shopping-after-911.htm

15   Foster, Richard. Celebration of Discipline; pg. 80.

16   Rohr, Richard. Simplicity; pg. 165.

17   Foster, Richard. Celebration of Discipline; pg.79.

18   W. H. Davies. *Leisure* (1911)

19   www.lexilogos.com/english/ancienthebrew.

20   The Northern Irish Conflict: A Chronology: http://www.infoplease.com/spot/northireland1

21   The Tea Party and Republican Conservatism

22   Chad Smith. *The Gainesville Sun*; September 12, 2010. Pastor Terry Jones does not possess a college degree of any sort. He is not seminary trained and received his honorary degree from an online school of theology that is not accredited (California Graduate School of Theology).

23   www.bbc.co.uk/news/world-south-asia-12949975.

24   http://motherjones.com/politics/2011/10/occupy-wall-street-international-origins?page=1

25   : http://endeavors.unc.edu/occupy

26   Word invented for one of the opening slogans of the OWS movement: "Democracy, not Corporatocracy."

27   www.nycga.net/groups/visionandgoals; November 20,2011.

28   www.teapartypatriots.org/; November 25, 2011.

29   http://www.interfaithencounter.wordpress.com/

30   http://www.mujerfla.org/

[31] Allison and Kaye, *Strategic Planning for Non Profit Organizations*

[32] The name of the project has been altered to protect the identity and reputation of people connected with it.

[33] William Peters. *A Class Divided*. New Haven: Yale University Press, 1971.

[34] The *New York Times*, January 21, 2011; www.nytimes.com/2011/01/22/world/africa/22sidi.html?

[35] Anonymous narrative about unemployment in United States of America; www.jobsearch.about.com/u/sty/unemployment/unemploymentstories/99-weeks-and-over-2000-resumes-sent.htm (accessed November, 2011).

[36] www.cbsnews.com/8301-503544_162-57335118-503544/newt-gingrich-poor-kids-dont-work-unless-its-illegal/

[37] http://www.motherjones.com/politics/2012/09/secret-video-romney-private-fundraiser

[38] http://library.cqpress.com/cqresearcher/document.php?id=cqresrre1966032300

[39] http://publicreligion.org/research/2011/11/research-note-overwhelming-support-for-increasing-the-minimum-wage/

[40] National Center for Policy Analysis, August 2, 2011; www.ncpa.org/sub/dpd/index.php?Article_ID=20940.

[41] www.abs-cbnnews.com/lifestyle/11/18/11/pizza-vegetable-according-us-lawmakers; November 20, 2011.

[42] Lawrence Britt. "Fascism, Anyone?" www.secularhumanism.org/library/fi/britt_23_2.htm.

[43] http://www.splcenter.org/get-informed/intelligence-files/ideology/neo-nazi/the-neo-nazi-movement/

44   http//www.theatlantic.com/business/archive/2012/03/why-is-the-gop-suddenly-turning-against-college/254337

45   http://www.rushlimbaugh.com/daily/2011/10/27/dittoheads_on_higher_education

46   http//s3.amazonaws.com/texasgop_pre/assets/original/2012Platform_Final.pdf

47   http://maddowblog.msnbc.com/_news/2011/03/08/6217859-rick-scott-and-tax-cuts-for-dummies?lite

48   http://www.heraldtribune.com/article/20120618/opinion/306189999?p=3&tc=pg

49   Htttp://abusergoestowork.com/tag/carlos-beruff/

50   http://politics.heraldtribune.com/2011/10/12/rick-scotts-desire-to-cut-liberal-arts-funding-raises-eyebrows-at-university-of-florida/

51   Alan K. L. Chan, (ed.). *Mencius: Contexts and Interpretations.* Honolulu: University of Hawaii Press, 2002.

52   www.globalissues.org/article/53/pharmaceutical-corporations-and-aids.

53   http://annonc.oxfordjournals.org/content/10/11/1261.full.pdf.

54   Actuarial Society of South Africa (2011, 9th March) "ASSA AIDS Model 2008 Media Release."

55   Gustavo Gutierrez. *Essential Writings.* New York: Orbis Books, 1996.

Made in the USA
Lexington, KY
19 January 2013